Comparing Learning Systems:

the good, the bad, the ugly, and the counter-productive

by Roland Meighan

with a foreword by Michael Foot

And why many home-based educating families have found a learning system which is fit for a democracy

Educational Heretics Press

Published 2005 by Educational Heretics Press
113 Arundel Drive, Bramcote, Nottingham NG9 3FQ

British Cataloguing in Publication Data

Meighan, Roland
Comparing Learning Systems: the good, the bad, the ugly, and the
counter-productive

ISBN   1-900219-28-X

Design and production: Educational Heretics Press

Cover design by Educational Heretics Press

Printed by Mastaprint Plus Ltd.,
Stuart House, 5/7 Wellington St., Long Eaton, Nottingham NG10 4LY

Contents

Dedication

Foreword by Michael Foot

Chapter 1   An introduction to the study of
             learning systems   1

Chapter 2   Authoritarian learning systems   9

Chapter 3   Autonomous learning systems   15

Chapter 4   Democratic learning systems   37

Chapter 5   Interactionist learning systems   57

Chapter 6   The next learning system   77

Chapter 7   'What is and what might be':
             personalised education as learner-
             managed learning instead of
             government-directed learning   93

Chapter 8   Conclusion: why not move to a
             learning system fit for a
             democracy?   99

This book is dedicated to the memory of my aunt
Gwen Collett née Moore
who never achieved fame for anything, but was just a
special human being.

Other books by Roland Meighan

Roland Meighan began writing for public consumption in his mid-thirties
because it was a requirement of his appointment as a university lecturer.
He was, until recently, a long-standing editor of the influential journal
Educational Review and author or co-author of over a hundred
publications, including twelve books. Two of them, *Perspectives on
Society* and *A Sociology of Educating,* have become best-selling, classic
texts.

Other well-known works of his are:
Flexischooling: Education for Tomorrow Starting Yesterday;
an edited work entitled *Learning From Home-based Education;*
Theory and Practice of Regressive Education;
a book of educational quotations entitled *The Freethinkers' Guide to the
Educational Universe;*
a directory to alternative ideas entitled *The Freethinkers' Pocket
Directory to the Educational Universe;*
and *Natural Learning and the Natural Curriculum.*

His most recent works are *John Holt: Personalised Education and the
Reconstruction of Schooling,* written as a tribute to the work of Holt, and
Damage Limitation: trying to reduce the harm schools do to children.
He has written for journals, for book publishers, for magazine readers
and for newspapers, for a variety of audiences including parents,
students, academics and anyone interested in educational ideas. His
work has been translated into more than twelve languages.

Foreword

At the school of which I am a governor, we were told recently that vandalism has declined. Such satisfaction that this news might have occasioned, however, was marred, for me at least, by the news that the decline had coincided with the installation of CCTV in strategically important parts of the school. Such is an example of the present reality of schooling in West Norfolk.

In his recent annual report, the Chief Inspector of Schools records a worrying deterioration in behaviour in schools. He also says that, judged by Ofsted's criteria, there are more 'failing' schools than there were a year ago. Meanwhile, the National Audit Office reports that rates of truancy from our schools have risen to a disturbing degree. And in last year's Interim Report of his Working Group on 14-19 Reform, Sir Mike Tomlinson admitted that: *"High truancy rates and behavioural problems are evidence of significant disengagement (from school) at or before age 14"*. Such are examples of the present reality of schooling in England and Wales. They are examples which will be widely known because they have been widely reported. And they are, properly, matters of national concern.

I guess, though, that fewer people will know of another part of the present reality which is illustrated by a DfES guidance publication, issued in November 2004, entitled: *Getting more pupils to level 5 in science: Part 2 - A Year 9 toolkit for science departments.* Doesn't the heart sink at the very title!

But read the 'toolkit' and experience a pummelling of the spirit. Read, for example, page 7 where it states that: *"Scientific answers are always required. For example, 'absorbed' should be used, not 'vanished'; 'evaporate' not 'dry up'. Other common non-scientific expressions often result in no marks being given"*. So: for a child to understand and to describe the process by which a puddle dries up counts for nothing unless he uses the word 'evaporate'.

Which would be disturbing enough, but consider also what appears just a little earlier on that same page 7: *"It is important to tell pupils that they should always attempt these questions even if they are unsure of the answer. A good guess can gain valuable marks"*. So: a guess could gain a mark - but understanding will not, unless the correct scientific terminology is used!

Such are examples of the scarcely credible reality of life in our schools today - the local and the national, the well known and the less well known. It is a reality that government ministers and their apologists seek to hide behind a smokescreen of improved test results. But the fault lines and the flaws of the reality demand a response in terms which address their essence. It is a response which politicians and policy makers remain reluctant to acknowledge, let alone attempt.

Which is why we must remain grateful to Roland Meighan for his provocative and searching contributions over many years to the national debate about education. In particular now, he deserves our thanks for this latest of his books, *Comparing Learning Systems* – as provocative and searching as ever. He ends it with a challenge: *"Let's be a bit bolder than trying to make yesterday's tired and failed ideas of mass schooling work!"*

The validity and the urgency of that challenge should be clear to all. But this book goes much further than merely confirming validity and urgency. In fact, it is full of pointers towards how best to meet that challenge, how best to do so in ways that address root causes rather than superficial symptoms.

Thus it is that *Comparing Learning Systems* is a most positive contribution to the debate about present unsatisfactory state of education. It points the way towards something which is much better for our children and our society than that which presently constrains and obstructs and thereby ill-serves.

Roland would not expect everybody to agree with everything he suggests. But I *would* expect everybody who is concerned about the well-being of our children and our society to benefit from exposure to his thinking and his insights.

Michael W Foot
February 2005

Michael Foot retired from a primary headship in 1995 having taught in primary schools in Gloucestershire, Buckinghamshire and Norfolk.

Chapter one

An introduction to the study of learning systems

You probably know more about learning systems than you think. And there are more of them than you think. Here is a list of some familiar ones:

playgroups, nursery, infants, junior, secondary school, further education college, traditional universities, the Open University, the University of the Third Age, early childhood 'natural learning' at home, home-based education, Scouts, Guides, Woodcraft Folk, Duke of Edinburgh Award Scheme, the Public Library, learning clubs for Judo, Table Tennis, Tennis, Athletics, Dance, etc., Book Circles, learning co-operatives, community learning centres, the Army, Suicide Bombers Camps, and Terrorist Schools. Then there are schools, varying from the Danish EFTA residential model, to the City as School 'school without walls' approach, to the Summerhill democratic version, to that of the radical Sudbury Valley School, USA, to Canadian Cyber-schools, to Virtual Schools to Flexi-colleges. Classifying this variety of learning systems is part of the task of this book.

As a young teacher, I came across the following learning league table from National Training Laboratories, Bethel, Maine USA It was an attempt to rank a number of learning systems according to how much the learners remembered afterwards.

	Average retention rate
Formal teaching	5%
Reading	10%
Audio-visual	20%
Demonstration	30%
Discussion Group	50%
Practice by doing	75%
Teaching others	90%
Immediate use of learning	90%

This helped set in motion my life-long interest in learning systems. (See *A Sociology of Educating*, fourth edition 2003, which could easily have been entitled *The Study of Learning Systems.*) Five key propositions emerged from my investigations.

1. There exists a variety of learning systems and each one produces different results.

Bertrand Russell in *On Education* (p.28) states the problem like this:

> *"We must have some concept of the kind of person we wish to produce before we can have any definite opinion as to the education which we consider best."*

So, first decide your intentions, then choose an appropriate learning system - the one that is 'fit for purpose'. Thus, if we adopt the view that the world's most pressing need is to produce people who will,
(a) do no harm to each other,
(b) do no harm to the environment,
(c) do no harm to oneself,
(d) and maybe even do a little good in the world,
learning based on co-operation has to replace that based on competition. We can go on to say more than this – we need people who are capable, confident researchers and democratically competent, in order to achieve these aims.

If these are our intentions, then we will need to design a learning system that gives us the best chance of achieving them. It needs to be 'fit for purpose'.

The first learning system we actually encounter when young, is the natural learning system of the home where,

i. Parents soon find out that young children are **natural learners**. They are like explorers or research scientists busily gathering information and making meaning out of the world. Most of this learning is not the result of teaching, but rather a constant and universal learning activity as natural as breathing.

ii. Our brains are **programmed to learn** unless discouraged. A healthy brain stimulates itself by interacting with what it finds interesting or challenging in the world around it.

iii. Our brains learn from any mistakes and operate a **self-correcting process.**

iv. We parents achieve the amazing feats of helping our children to talk, walk and make sense of the home and the environment in which it is set, by **responding to this natural learning process.** All this is achieved, with varying degrees of success, by us so-called amateurs - the parent or parents, and other care-givers such as grandparents. What we discover as parents is that, if supported and encouraged, children will not only begin to make sense of their world, but can also acquire the attitudes and skills necessary for successful learning throughout their lives.

v. But, this process of natural learning can be **hindered or halted by insensitive adult interference.** If this causes children to lose confidence in their natural learning and its self correcting features, and instead, learn to be dependent on others to 'school' their minds, the results can be stultifying. E. T. Hall, writing in 1977, declared that, in the USA,

> *"Schools have transformed learning from one of the most rewarding of all human activities into a painful, boring, dull, fragmenting, mind-shrinking, soul-shrivelling experience."*

A prize-winning New York teacher, John Taylor Gatto, describes this kind of schooling as training children,

> *"... to be obedient to a script written by remote strangers ... Education demands you write the script of your own life with the help of people who love or care about you."*

The Natural Curriculum

The 'natural' curriculum is the 'course of study' that humans develop as fast as physical and other conditions permit. So, babies accumulate knowledge through activities such as play, imitation, and interaction with any adults around. Play is best seen as children's work, as their research: one grandparent noted recently that her granddaughter, at the end of a drinks and chat break, suddenly said, *"I must get on with my play-work now."*

The content of this natural curriculum is a **set of existential questions**. They include:

Who am I?
Who are you?
Who are they?
Where do we belong?
Who gets what?
How do we find out?
Where are we going?
How am I doing?
Who decides what?
What is fair, right or just?

It is a set of questions that stays with us permanently with the answers being reviewed constantly throughout our lives, as we assemble our tool-kit of knowledge, in what Jerome Bruner once described as a 'spiral curriculum'. From time to time, we may engage with those attempts at systematic bodies of knowledge called subjects, to help with some answers to these questions.

The question, *'Who am I?'* will be redefined many times. As people pass through the roles of infant, child, adolescent, young adult, single person, couple, married person, parent, older person, their self-concepts have to be revised.

When young children reach five, they are asking, on average, 30 questions an hour. At this stage, one provisional answer to the question of *'How do we find out?'* has been gained, by achieving competence in the mother tongue. Until quite recently in human history, this natural curriculum was sufficient to keep most of us going throughout life. But then, about 150 years ago, an institution called the compulsory school was introduced, and suddenly, the natural curriculum was displaced to be replaced by an imposed curriculum based on the government's questions, the government's required answers, and the government's required assessment. The message is dramatically changed:

*"Your experience, your concerns, your hopes, your fears, your desires, your interests, they count for nothing. What counts is what **we** are interested in, what **we** care about, and what **we** have decided you are to learn."*
John Holt, in *The Underachieving School*, p. 161

2. How do you classify learning systems?

Since there are many learning systems, some means of classifying them would be helpful for the purposes of comparison. None of the attempts I looked at seemed to be getting us very far. (See *A Sociology of Educating*, Continuum books, fourth edition 2003 for an account of some of them.) Here is the approach I devised which classified systems as Authoritarian, Autonomous and Democratic, along with a fourth category of Interactive.

The Authoritarian View of Education, or, *"You will do it our way"*

In **authoritarian education**, in its various forms, one person, or a small group of people, make and implement the decisions about what to learn, when to learn, how to learn, how to assess learning, and the learning environment. This is often all decided before the learners are recruited as individuals or meet as a group. As an exclusive method, it is favoured by totalitarian regimes because it aims to produce the conformist, lockstep mentality. Teachers can easily learn to see themselves as 'miserable rule-followers', as one teacher put it.

The Autonomous View of Education, or, *"I did it my way"*

In **autonomous education**, the decisions about learning are made by the individual learners. Each one manages and takes responsibility for his or her learning programmes. Individuals may seek advice or look for ideas about what to learn and how to learn it by research or by consulting others. They do not have to re-invent the culture, but interact with it. As an exclusive method it is favoured by liberal or libertarian regimes.

The Democratic View of Education, or, *"We did it our way"*

In **democratic education**, the learners as a group have the power to make most, or even all, of the key decisions, since power is shared and not appropriated in advance by a minority of one or more. Democratic countries might be expected to favour this approach, but such educational practices are rare and often meet with sustained, hostile and irrational opposition.

The Interactive View of Education, or, *"We did it in a variety of ways"*

In the **interactive** **approach** to **education**, the authoritarian, democratic and autonomous ideologies are used in a variety of patterns. They may be alternated, or revolved or used in some order of ranking.

In what follows, a chapter is devoted to a brief account of each of these types. A case study, or several case studies, are then attached.

3.   A key lesson from the study of learning systems is that *how* you learn is as important, if not more important than *what* you learn.

The **manner** of learning is as critical as the learning itself. Thus it assumed that literacy is automatically good. **But, learning literacy in a bully institution makes you a literate bully.** The survivor of a concentration camp had this to say on the matter.

"Reading, writing and arithmetic are important only if they serve to make our children more human."

As governments world-wide bang the drum for more education, Don Glines of 'Educational Futures Projects', USA, introduces a sobering thought:

"... the majority of the dilemmas facing society have been perpetrated by the best traditional college graduates: environmental pollution; political ethics; have/have not gap; under-employment - (in fact) the sixty four micro-problems which equal our one macro-problem!"

So, if some of the high achievers are responsible for the various major problems the world faces, perhaps we need less 'education' and more 'wisdom'? Some of our most revered institutions may be more 'part of the problem, than part of the solution'.

The US radical, Nat Needle, writes in response to former President Bill Clinton's call to US citizens to prepare themselves to compete in the most ruthless century yet:

"... if the 21st century becomes the story of human beings around the world pitted against each other in a struggle for well-being, even survival, this will only be because we failed to imagine something better and insist on it for ourselves and our children.

"I don't care to motivate my children by telling them that they will have to be strong to survive the ruthless competition. I'd rather tell them that the world needs their wisdom, their talents, and their kindness, so much so that the possibilities for a life of service are without limits of any kind. I'd like to share with them the open secret that this is the path to receiving what one needs in a lifetime, and to becoming strong. "

(AERO-Gramme, No. 25, Fall 1998)

Nat Needle is asking for a different kind of learning system to achieve quite different purposes.

4. Choosing to operate a mass, coercive, standardised learning system inevitably stifles variety in achievement and limits the amount of high achievement.

Sir Christopher Ball puts it like this:

"Unfortunately in the 20th-century ... we have been too ready to classify people as bright or dim. This has conspired to hide the truth that anyone who can speak their mother tongue, drive a car, and understand the offside rule in football is highly talented and capable of great feats of learning. Human potential is not in short supply. "

(Christopher Ball, *RSA Journal* 4/4 1999)

To some extent, the regime I often found when studying the home-based education learning system has characteristics reminiscent of those found by the Smithsonian research into the learning regimes of the **'genius'**. McCurdy of the University of North Carolina identified three key factors:

(i). a high degree of individual attention given by parents and other adults and expressed in a variety of educational activities, accompanied by abundant affection,

(ii). only limited contact with other children outside the family but plenty of contact with supportive adults, (iii). an environment rich in, and supportive of, imagination and fantasy.

McCurdy came to a shocking conclusion. It was that the mass education system of the USA based on formal methods, coercion and inflexible organisation, constituted a vast experiment in reducing all these three factors to the minimum. The result was the suppression of high achievement. Home-based education is one learning system capable of re-instating these key factors.

The choice of a learning system is not, therefore, a trivial matter since it can have significant effects. Edmond Holmes, chief inspector of schools in the early 1900s, thought that the UK government was backing a loser:

> "... with the best of intentions, the leading actors in it, the parents and teachers of each successive generation, so bear themselves as to entail never-ending calamities on the whole human race - not the sensational calamities which dramatists love to depict, but inward calamities which are the deadlier for their very unobtrusiveness, for our being so familiar with them that we accept them at last as our appointed lot - such calamities as perverted ideals, debased standards, contracted horizons, externalised aims, self-centred activities, weakened will-power, lowered vitality, restricted and distorted growth, and (crowning and summarising the rest) a profound misconception of the meaning of life."

5. The next learning system will need to offer 'alternatives for everybody, all the time' (just as most home-based educators do already)

In my earlier book, *The Next Learning System*, the ten or so time switches of change that will move learning systems into more fluid patterns are given. These ideas will be examined in chapter six of this book.

Chapter two

Authoritarian learning systems

Authoritarian systems of learning, in their various forms, have one person, or a small group of people, making and implementing the decisions about what to learn, when to learn, how to learn, how to assess learning, and the nature of the imposed learning environment. These decisions are taken in course planning committees and accreditation boards often long before the learners are recruited as individuals or meet as a group. Its slogan is usually summed up in the words:

"You will do it our way – or else ..."

Discipline
is defined as learning to obey the rules and instructions decided by the management.

Knowledge
is defined as, essentially, information contained in the traditional subjects.

Learning
is defined as listening to subject experts and reading their books.

Teaching
is defined as uninvited formal instruction by trained or approved adults.

Parents
are expected, for the most part, to be spectators, preferably admiring of the 'experts'.

Resources
are defined as, predominately, subject textbooks.

Location
is a central place (school) where the experts (teachers) can easily be assembled together cheaply, with large groups of pupils.

Organisation
is usually in age-stratified classes formally arranged.

Assessment
is, mostly, by tests of how well pupils can repeat the subject matter.

Aims are, essentially, to produce mini-academic subject experts, with those who fail in this enterprise required to be useful in industry or commerce.

Power
is in the hands of the appointed individual or a senior management team or governors who believe that they have the right to impose their decisions on others.

In authoritarian systems, one person, or a group of people, exercises dominance over other people although the form of this dominance varies. This can range from outright coercion through fear, to deference to rank or believed expertise, to persuasion through controlled communication, through to consultation initiated by those in power entirely on their terms. In contrast, in a democratic system of learning, power is shared to some degree or other. Authoritarian thinking about learning leads, sooner or later, to an imposed National Curriculum and other compulsory features.

It is the general approach favoured by totalitarian systems, whether right-wing fascist, or left-wing communist, or religious for the imposition of a particular religious doctrine. '*You will do it our way!*' applies whether it is a political, economic, social or religious set of dogmas. Visitors from societies that have been totalitarian see it at once. When in 1989 I asked Professor Eugenia Potulicka from Poland what she would say in her report about schools in the UK and the imposition of the second National Curriculum on our education system, she said: "*Oh, I shall tell them it is totalitarian.*" She went on to say: "*The 1988 Education Act is a very dangerous development for it has politicised schooling in the direction of fascist thinking. It is the worst development in Europe at the moment.*"

School, based on the current model of compulson, is centred on domination and can therefore be seen as a *bully institution.* Next it employs a *bully curriculum* - the compulsory National Curriculum. This is enforced by the increasingly favoured *bully pedagogy* of teacher-directed formal teaching. Currently, this is reinforced by the *bully compulsory assessment system.* This system is enforced by a *bully inspectorate.* The unwritten, but powerful message of this package, is that: '*adults get their way by bullying'.* The answer to the question of how bullying arises in the mass schooling system, is that it is built into the model itself.

There are at least three types of general outcome. The 'successful' pupils grow up to be officially sanctioned bullies in dominant authority positions as assertive politicians, doctors, teachers, civil servants, journalists and the like. A majority of the 'less successful' learn to accept the mentality of the bullied - the submissive and dependent mind-set of people who need someone to tell them what to think and do. They must learn to 'know their place'. A third outcome is the production of a group of free-lance bullies who rebel against knowing their place, become troublesome and end up in trouble of varying degree of seriousness.

But the present authoritarian approach to schooling has been described by Holt (1977) in *Growing Without Schooling*, No. 17, p.8, as regimental:

"School is the Army for kids. Adults make them go there, and when they get there, adults tell them what to do, bribe and threaten them into doing it, and punish them when they don't."

One growing reaction to this domination-centred approach has been the rapid growth of home-based education, especially in the USA, Canada, New Zealand, Australia and the UK. Democratic practice and its consequences are more likely to be encountered than in the mass, coercive schooling system, because power is usually shared with the learners who have more and more say in the decision-making. Consequently, they usually develop confidence in managing their own learning in co-operation with members of the family and others.

Further analysis of the concept of authoritarian learning systems can be found in Meighan, R. and Blatchford, I., *A Sociology of Educating*, Continuum books, fourth edition 2003.

Case Study:

The 2nd (1988) National Curriculum for England and Wales

(The text below above is a lightly edited version from two sources to be found on www.parentcentre.gov.uk and www.parents.org.uk)

The National Curriculum for England and Wales 1988 is described by the government as a blueprint to be used by schools to try to ensure that teaching standards are universally consistent. Schools are allowed to plan how the National Curriculum fits in with their particular strengths and introduce other activities that extend the learning experience for their pupils. The National Curriculum:

- sets out the most important knowledge and skills that every child has the right to learn, as selected by the government,

- is a flexible framework required of teachers by government, so that all school children are taught in a way that is balanced and manageable, but stretching enough to challenge them and meet their diverse needs,

- gives standards that measure how well children are doing in each subject – so teachers can celebrate achievement and plan to help them do even better.

The National Curriculum was re-introduced in 1988 to ensure that all children in State schools receive the same basic education. (Private schools and home-based educated children are exempt.)

Ten subjects must be taught in primary schools and they are:

> English
> Maths
> Science
> IT (Information Technology)
> History
> Geography
> Design Technology
> Art
> Music
> Physical Education

Religious Education, though not listed, is considered part of the basic curriculum and must be taught in all schools in England.

Skills, Understanding and Knowledge

In each of the ten subjects, children are taught Skills, Understanding and Knowledge.

- Skills – these are things the children need to be able to do, for instance, how to weigh things accurately using a set of scales; how to tell the time; how to look things up in a dictionary.

- Understanding – this means having a grasp of basic concepts and ideas, such as, writing conveys meaning; water, ice and steam are all forms of the same substance; the difference between living, dead and non-living.

- Knowledge – this means knowing things 'off by heart', for example, historical dates, countries in Europe, how to spell common words. So, your child might have the skill of being able to multiply 8 by 6, know that they equal 48, and understand that multiplication is a process of repeated addition.

Progression

Although your child will move through school year by year, the National Curriculum required by the government says when things must be taught by devising segments called Key Stages. (In the first National Curriculum of the late 1800s and early 1900s, these were called Standards.) For example, Key Stage One covers what a child aged from 5 to 7 years should know. Key Stage Two covers what a child aged from 7 to 11 years should know. How does it all work?

Age	Stage	Year	Tests
3-4	Foundation		
4-5		Year R	Baseline assessment
5-6	Key Stage One	Year 1	
6-7		Year 2	National tests
7-8	Key Stage Two	Year 3	
8-9		Year 4	
9-10		Year 5	
10-11		Year 6	National tests
11-12	Key Stage 3	Year 7	
12-13		Year 8	
13-14		Year 9	National tests
14-15	Key Stage 4	Year 10	Some children take GCSEs
15-16		Year 11	Most children take GCSEs or other national qualifications

(The National Curriculum to be found in other countries varies considerably from this pattern. Some have just two pages of recommendations, some include other subjects such as logic, philosophy and social science.)

Chapter three

Autonomous learning systems

In **autonomous education**, the decisions about learning are made by the individual learners. They manage and take responsibility for their own learning programmes. They may seek advice from others or look for ideas about what to learn and how to learn it by research and consultation. Its slogan is usually summed up in the words:

"I did it my way   though not ignoring any useful advice, support and encouragement from the people around me."

Discipline
is that form known as self-discipline.

Knowledge
is, essentially, the repertoire of learning and research skills needed to cope with new ideas.

Learning
is, mostly, self-directed activity and personal research in order to gain experience, information or skills.

Teaching
is, usually, self-teaching; the purpose of other teachers is to teach you how to teach yourself better, and the learner may invite such teaching at will, but 'uninvited teaching' is rarely legitimate.

Parents
are expected to be part of the team supporting the learner's development in learning skills and confidence.

Resources
are, predominately, first-hand experiences as the basis of personal research backed up by any other resources seen to be appropriate.

Location
is anywhere that useful or interesting learning can take place.

Organisation
is often in individual learning stations in institutional settings, but remains flexible to match the variety of learner-managed tasks.

Assessment
is, commonly, by self-assessment using any tests, devised by the learner or by others, that are seen to be appropriate to the situation.

Aims

are, essentially, to produce people with the confidence and skills to manage their own learning throughout their entire lives.

Power

is seen as devolved to individuals who are seen as morally responsible for the exercise of their autonomy.

Autonomous learning incorporates or overlaps with a number of other ideas. One is that of being autodidactic or self-taught. Another is that of self-managed learning and learner-managed learning. Then there is individualised learning, provided that the learner has considerable involvement in the planning - if the teacher plans it, it is authoritarian. Finally, there is personalised learning, of the kind advocated by *Personalised Education Now* (PEN – the trading name for the Centre for Personalised Education Trust). PEN maintains that people learn best:

• when they are self-motivated and are equipped with learning to learn tools ·

• when they take responsibility for their own lives and learning

• when they feel comfortable in their surroundings, free from coercion and fear

• when educators and learners value, trust, respect and listen to each other

• when education is seen as an active life-long process

A common confusion is to mistake autonomous learning with a laissez-faire approach to learning where learners are left to their own devices, without a framework of support, encouragement, example or incentives. Leaving learners purely to their own devices is not a learning system and so is not analysed in this book. The writings of Rouseau make a case for this approach.

In contrast, Professor Ian Cunningham of the *Centre for Self Managed Learning* in Brighton, declares that we need to provide an appropriate structure to give real freedom to students as they work out what they want to learn, how they want to do it, and how they can achieve their goals in life. Support, that is, but not control. (See also the case study of its offshoot, the *South Downs Learning Centre* in chapter six)

The first case study of autonomous learning that follows is that of home-based education. .

Case study:

Home-based education

Autonomous education is more frequently found in home-based education than in almost any other context – a rival being the public library system, the subject of the second case study. Many home-educating families start with 'school at home' with timetables, courses and textbooks. Some continue this way but most, in the UK at least, review their progress, and move to more and more learner-managed learning. A major difference between homes and school is in the method of learning. Schools use a great deal of formal instruction, an approach, as we saw earlier with about 5% - 25% effectiveness, whereas learning at home uses a great deal of purposive conversation (discussion) with a 50% plus level of effectiveness.

(a) Natural learning and 'dovetailing'

Families educating at home often engage in highly sophisticated activity without necessarily being able to articulate what they are doing. Most parents find, as John Holt proposed in *Learning All the Time,* that young children are 'natural' learners. As noted in the introduction, they are like explorers or research scientists busily gathering information and making meaning out of the world. Most of this learning is not the result of teaching, but rather a constant and universal learning activity 'as natural as breathing'. Parents achieve the remarkable feats of helping their children to walk and talk by responding to this process. This is, perhaps, the most successful example of educational practice world-wide. In the first five years of life, astonishing learning takes place as a non-verbal infant learns its native language, to walk and to achieve competence within its home and local environment. All this achieved, with varying degrees of success, by so-called amateurs - the parent or parents and other care-givers such as grandparents.

The highly sophisticated activity of parents is described as 'dovetailing' into the child's behaviour. Parents appear to have no pre-determined plan of language teaching, they simply respond to the cues provided and give support to the next stage of learning as the child decides to encounter it.

(b) Direct access to an information-rich society

When schools were set up we lived in an information-poor society. Therefore getting children together in one place to give them access made some kind of sense. Now that we live in an information-rich society, it makes little or no sense, as Richard North (1987) observes:

"*We no longer have to force-feed education to children: they live in a world in which they are surrounded by educative resources. There are around 500 hours each of the schools' television and radio every year in this country. There are several million books in public libraries. There are museums in every town. There is a constant flow of cheap or free information from a dozen media. There are home computers which are easily connected to phones and thus other computers ... There are thousands of work-places ... There are ... the old, the disabled, the very young all in need of children in their lives, all in need of the kind of help caring and careful youngsters can give, and all of them rich sources of information about the world, and freely available to any child who isn't locked away in school.*"

Although the information-rich society is a world-wide phenomenon, some societies in the 'majority world' are still relatively information-poor. The implications of home-based education are less clear in these circumstances. Yet the arrival of high-tech clockwork radios and ultimately computers, is likely to be a significant breakthrough here, where power supplies are a problem.

(c) The adaptation to a wide variety of learning styles

Given the fact that we are able to locate over thirty differences in individual learning styles, any uniform approach to the curriculum or to learning is intellectual death to some, and often most, of the learners, and is therefore suspect.

Human beings, adults and children alike, differ from each other quite dramatically in learning styles. To date, thirty-two such differences have been catalogued (Keefe, 1987). An example would be the difference between those who learn better with some background noise and those who learn better in quiet conditions. Individuals also differ in the kind of light conditions, temperature conditions, bodily positions, food intake and type of companions needed for efficient learning. Bio-chronology is another factor, for some are early-day learners and some late-day or evening/night learners.

Therefore, the situation in which one teacher faces thirty children in one room and is required to deliver the same material within a given period of time, say forty five minutes, to all of them, means that drastic harm to the quality of learning of many of the class, and the resultant loss of a great deal of potential learning, is inevitable. In contrast, in the home-based education I have witnessed, the families rather take it for granted that learning styles differ, and vary the learning situations accordingly.

(d) Efficient use of time

When I have interviewed children who have come out of school into home-based education, I have asked them to compare the two experiences. Usually the first response is the comment on efficiency of learning. They say that they have frequently learnt more by coffee-time at home than in a whole day at school, so that the rest of the day is 'additional learning'. This helps explain why children who are 'behind' at school soon catch up at home, and also why they can end up two to ten years ahead of their schooled counterparts.

(e) A non-hostile learning environment

It is not just efficiency that the children note. They have told me about the relaxed atmosphere at home which encourages them to be increasingly confident in taking over the management of their own learning. When they started school at five years of age, we know they were asking about thirty knowledge or enquiry questions an hour, but that this soon drops and eventually gets to around zero. In non-hostile home-based education, they tell me their interest in learning and curiosity and questioning begins to build up again.

By contrast, the main effects of the 1988 Education Reform Act in the UK have been to create many more hostile learning situations. It is hardly necessary to argue the point - almost every newspaper, radio station and television channel carries reports each week of school exclusions, unhappy children, unhappy parents, and teachers queuing up to take early retirement. John Holt even forecast that this might happen in 1975:

> "A majority want the schools to be even more rigid, threatening, and punitive than they are, and they will probably become so."
>
> (Escape from Childhood, p.58)

Once, when I ran a day course for student teachers on 'alternative ideas in education and the next learning system', the gathering was very subdued from the start. Then the story began to unfold. Not one of the students wanted to go into schools and develop a career in teaching because of the way the task had been presented to them in the previous months in terms of the National Curriculum. *"I just do not want to go into schools and do the things to children I have been ordered to do"* one student volunteered. The others agreed. The task had been presented in terms of what C. Wright Mills described as the 'cultural mechanics' task - to bolt on to children bits of selected information and then test whether they had stuck on.

This echoes the verdict on the previous UK National Curriculum of the late 1800s which ran for about thirty years. Its designer was the Senior Chief Inspector, Edmond Holmes. When he retired he wrote a book condemning the whole of his previous thirty years' work. Holmes observed that under a National Curriculum approach, learning and teaching became mechanical because,

"the teacher is engaged in laying thin films of information on the surface of the child's mind and then after a brief interval he is skimming these off in order to satisfy himself that they have been duly laid."

The 1988 UK National Curriculum looks very much like the 1870s version both in subjects and in the 'tell them and test them' methodology.

(f) Learner-managed learning: plan, do, review

The success of the Ipsilanti High Scope programme has been widely publicised. Children in schools using this approach are encouraged in the basic skills of deep learning; that is, they learn to plan, do and review. What has been overlooked is that home-based education usually operates to the same principles and is therefore equally successful in producing competent and confident learners. By adding the efficiency factor mentioned above, however, the home-based pupils are likely to pull ahead.

John Holt, in *Teach Your Own*, lists some of the principles he has observed and advocates in the learning approach of parents who are home-based educators:

"For a long, long time, people who were good at sharing what they knew have realised certain things: (1) to help people learn something, you must first understand what they already know; (2) showing people how to do something is better than telling them and letting them do it

is best of all; (3) you mustn't tell or show too much at once, since people digest new ideas slowly and must feel secure with new skills or knowledge before they are ready for more; (4) you must give people as much time as they want and need to absorb what you have shown or told them; (5) instead of testing their understanding with questions you must let them show how much or how little they understand by the questions they ask you; (6) you must not get impatient or angry when people do not understand; (7) scaring people only blocks learning , and so on. " (p.52)

(g) The use of the Catalogue Curriculum approach

At least six different types of curriculum can be identified. The logistics of each of these types has been outlined elsewhere (Meighan, 1988, 1993). All the various types of curriculum can be on offer at the same time in the **Catalogue Curriculum.** Others may have used this description before, but I have not come across it. Don Glines has something similar in his 'window-shopping' approach to the curriculum, and the 'shopper's guide' for students in his *Creating Educational Futures* (McNaughton and Gunn, Michigan 1995).

The learners, whether in schools full-time, or in flexi-time schooling plans, or full-time home-based education, are offered a catalogue of learning opportunities. The catalogue may be printed out for scrutiny or just made available, and it includes a variety of approaches:

* set courses, of the National Curriculum kind,
* ideas for making your own courses,
* instructions as to how to set up a learning co-operative,
* self-instructional packages,
* ways of getting access to other available learning resources and opportunities.

This approach to curriculum has been adopted by most families for their children between the ages of nought and five and by many families in their home-based educational alternative to schools after the age of five.

A Catalogue Curriculum approach is adopted by all the families I have researched myself. Without being able to articulate the theory, they utilise a variety of elements in their programmes. Often the morning programme may be imposed and pre-planned, sometimes to satisfy the wishes of the Local Education Officers, sometimes for external examination purposes, and sometimes for reasons of the family's own. The afternoon programme may then be of another kind; consultative, negotiated, or democratic in co-operation with another family. These families have already field-tested the Catalogue Curriculum.

An essential part of the approach of the families working in these flexible ways is the regular monitoring and evaluation of their curriculum. In some cases I have seen this taking place regularly and deliberately at morning coffee breaks supplemented by reviews at meal times. In other cases the planning and review has taken place in a regular Sunday evening meeting to decide the learning programme in outline for the following week.

(h) Matching the logic of Multiple Intelligence Theory

The case for the Catalogue Curriculum can be linked to recent research into learning. Howard Gardner in *The Unschooled Mind* identifies at least seven types of intelligence. Charles Handy in *The Age of Unreason* suggests that there are more than this. We have known for many years that there are more than thirty learning styles in humans. For these and other reasons, traditional education with its model of schooling devised in the age of the coach and horses, is obsolete. Most of the public debate about education can be likened to trying to make the stagecoach go faster by fixing roller-skates to the hooves of the horses.

The flexibility that a full-blown Catalogue Curriculum approach implies is now widely recognised as the way forward in order:

- to equip individuals so that they can cope with a rapidly changing world, creatively and imaginatively, rather than with fear, obstructionism and fatalism,

- to match the wide variety of individual learning styles, learning biographies, forms of intelligence and learner aspirations,

- to match the needs of the modern economy for flexible, capable and adaptable people,

- to match the needs of a modern, living democracy for people who can operate as participating citizens exercising responsible, informed choice, and acting with all the necessary possible positive tolerance needed to make an open and diverse society work.

(i) Adults as learning agents, learning coaches, and learning site managers

When adults quiz parents about home-based education they often ask how one or two parents can replace the team of experts of a school staff. Apart from pointing out that we live in an information-rich society now, so that what the teachers know is available anyway, parents go on to describe themselves as 'fixers' or 'learning site managers' who help arrange the learning programme. They may also operate as learning coaches, or as fellow learners researching alongside their children, rather than as instructors. John Holt gives a useful summary of the qualities required:

> *"We can sum up very quickly what people need to teach their own children. First of all, they have to **like** them, enjoy their company, their physical presence, their energy, foolishness, and passion. They have to enjoy all their talk and questions, and enjoy equally trying to answer those questions. They have to think of their children as friends, indeed very close friends, have to feel happier when they are near and miss them when they are away. They have to trust them as people, respect their fragile dignity, treat them with courtesy, take them seriously. They have to feel in their own hearts some of their children's wonder, curiosity, and excitement about the world. And they have to have enough confidence in themselves, scepticism about experts, and willingness to be different from most people, to take on themselves the responsibility for their children's learning."*
>
> (Teach Your Own, p.57)

(j) Plenty of first-hand experience

The research studies quoted earlier indicate that first-hand experience is important in the approach of home-schoolers to learning. Thus, in the studies of the use of computers and of science explorations, those involved in home-based education just take it for granted that large amounts of first-hand experiences are essential to achieve effective learning. This may set the parents up in another role as transport managers:

> *"The parents' role in home-schooling is not to be the fount of all knowledge ... Our role is to be enthusiastic and experienced learners, role models for our children, providing support and advice - and transportation to the library."*

('British Columbia Home-schooler', in D. S. Smith, *Parent-generated Home Study in Canada*, p.70, 1993)

(k) The experience of the various forms of discipline

The three kinds of behavioural discipline follow the pattern of the learning systems analysis given earlier. They are:

(i).   **Authoritarian** - where order is based on rules imposed by adults. Power resides in an individual or group of leaders.

(ii). **Autonomous** - where order is based on self-discipline and self-imposed rational rules. Power resides with the individual.

(iii). **Democratic** - where order is based on rules agreed after rational discussion, i.e. based on evidence, human rights values and the logic of consequences. Power is shared amongst the people in the situation.

There has been a centuries-old debate about which of these three is the best system of discipline. It is now a sterile debate. The complexities of modern life are such that **all three types of discipline** have a place to play in the scheme of things. In some situations we need to be able to cope with **authoritarian discipline** and behaviour either by taking a lead or taking instructions. At other times we need to co-operate with others and behave with the **democratic discipline** of evolving and agreeing rules and then implementing and policing them collectively. Sometimes we need to be self-directing, take decisions for ourselves and act with **autonomous discipline**.

The same variety is found in knowledge disciplines. Sometimes we need to have memorised information using subject disciplines and at others to know the discipline of how to research to find knowledge. It follows that an effective education requires experience of all these approaches and an awareness when each one in turn is appropriate.

The experience of families educating at home has demonstrated how this can be achieved. The learners sometimes direct their own studies. At other times they work in co-operation with others, and on other occasions decide to submit to instruction. The parents occasionally act as instructors, and at other times as facilitators, sometimes as co-learners, and often as sources of encouragement.

As before, families may not be able to articulate the sophisticated nature of their activity. But only a few schools, mostly the best of the nursery and infant schools, can match either the discipline variety or the curriculum variety of a home-educating family.

(l) Social Skills obtained from the real world

In the previous chapter we noted that a considerable amount of the research into home-based education has looked at the social aspects. The findings are consistent in showing that the social skills, social maturity and emotional development of home-educated children are superior.

This raises the question of how the myth, that mass compulsory authoritarian schooling is a socially maturing experience, can be sustained any longer. The reality is that we have actually constructed and sustained at massive public expense a machine for keeping children artificially immature. This is achieved by consigning them to the influence of the equally immature minds and behaviours of members of their peer group, by imposition, for 15,000 hours, in an authoritarian organisation. Chris Shute (1993) has graphically described this as *Compulsory Schooling Disease: how children absorb fascist values.*

As noted in an earlier chapter, the result is that the bully mentality is produced. The problem with most discussions about bullying is that the root causes are overlooked. School, based on the current model of the compulsory day-detention centre, is itself a bully institution. Next it employs a bully curriculum - the compulsory National Curriculum. This is 'delivered' by the increasingly favoured bully pedagogy of teacher-dominated formal teaching, which in turn is reinforced by the bully compulsory testing system. All this requires a bully inspectorate. The unwritten, but powerful message of this package, is that *the adults get their way by bullying.* This bullying is by psychological and emotional coercion for the most part, but the call for physical bullying in the form of physical punishment is never far away.

There are at least three possible outcomes. The 'successful' pupils grow up to be officially sanctioned bullies in dominant authority positions as assertive politicians, doctors, teachers, civil servants, journalists and the like.

A majority of the 'less successful' learn to accept the mentality of the bullied - the submissive and dependent mind-set of people who need someone to tell them what to think and do. John Holt describes this as the school's general course in Practical Slavery.

A third outcome is the production of a group of free-lance bullies who become troublesome and end up in trouble of varying degrees of seriousness.

Amongst the reasons families give for starting home-based education is that of getting away from bullying. Sometimes this is bullying by teachers, sometimes by children, sometimes it is by both, and sometimes by the dulling effect of a whole oppressive school regime, in effect, bullying by the government. In typical fashion, the government decreed in 2004 that school uniform should be compulsory. (The existence of a uniform at all used to mystify many teachers and others from overseas that I hosted when I was working at the University of Birmingham.) What families may not articulate is the escape from the long term effects of exposure to the bully mentality, briefly outlined above, but examined at greater length in Chris Shute's book and in Alice Miller's *For Your Own Good.*

(m) We now know more about how the brain actually works

One of the groups to have taken these ideas seriously is Accelerated Learning Systems Ltd. In *Accelerated Learning for the 21st Century,* Colin Rose and Malcolm J. Nicholl provide a survey of the evidence in a chapter entitled, 'The Awesome Brain'. They then apply some of the research findings to the design of their learning materials:

> *"The objective of Accelerated Learning is to:*
> *a. Actively involve the emotional brain - thereby making things more memorable.*
> *b. Sychronise left and right brain activity.*
> *c. Mobilise all eight intelligences so that learning is accessible.*
> *d. Introduce moments of relaxation to allow consolidation to take place."*

I find it intriguing that the home-educated young people I have investigated, although they may have no knowledge of modern brain research, have already worked out some of the consequences in their practice. Often, they are already using most of the principles of accelerated learning in their learning programmes.

In their book, Colin Rose and Malcolm J. Nicholl stress the importance of confidence-building and self-esteem. One of the most notable features of home-based education is precisely such an outcome. When I have appeared on television or have made a radio broadcast in the company of home-educators, the presenters and staff have always remarked on the maturity, poise and self-confidence of the children.

But we do not have to rely on anecdotal evidence here, because the systematic studies in the USA and the UK demonstrate the same outcome. In a study of 259 families in Delaware, Vicki D. Tillman (1995) replicated the findings of an earlier study by Taylor in 1986 that:

"... the self-concept of home-schooled children was significantly higher ..."

Tillman notes that the home-based educating families in her study were not isolated but active, contributing members of society, even in their childhood. She concludes:

"If socialisation can be measured by good self-esteem, home-schoolers in the Delaware Valley are doing well."

Conclusion

If we look at the reasons why home-based education is so successful, we find that they are linked with the latest research findings on multiple intelligences, the insights of modern brain research, the consequences of the move into an information-rich society, and the direct access made possible by the new technology of the communications revolution. Many home-based educators are indeed blazing a trail to the next learning system, in demonstrating how a more flexible approach to learning works in a variety of dimensions, with considerable use of the principles of autonomous education.

Case study:

The Public Library

Home-based educating families make a bee-line for the one learner-friendly institution they know most about – the public library. The philosophy of the library is autonomous learning. It is assumed that learners, of whatever age, will manage their own learning.

Britain's first public lending library opened in Manchester just over 150 years ago, (in September 1852), an event so significant for literacy and democracy that Charles Dickens felt compelled to make the trip north. *"This is an institution knowing no sect, no party, and no distinction, nothing but the public want and the public good,"* he said in a speech at the formal inauguration.

Visiting the library is the fourth most popular pastime in the UK, after going to pubs, restaurants and takeaways. 58% of Britons are members of their local library borrowing some 480 million books per year. As regards value for money, it costs the price of a first class stamp per person per week. There are 4,160 libraries in the UK plus another 630 mobile libraries in use.

Part of the appeal is because it is an autonomous learning system that fits in well with a democracy. Mass coercive schooling, on the other hand, is anti-democratic. Even during the last century it was described as *"compulsory mis-education"* (Paul Goodman), *"the tragedy of education"* (Edmond Holmes) and *"the betrayal of youth"* (James Hemming). It was inspired by totalitarian not democratic societies, which is why it was so popular with Stalin and Hitler, and why it appeals to a whole range of 'control-freaks' in the UK, the USA and elsewhere.

A democratic learning system needs to get away from **domination** and its endless stream of uninvited teaching. Instead it needs to be personalised in the sense of being learner-managed, based on invitation and encouragement and, if we actually believe in life-long learning, non-ageist. It needs to be democratic in at least three aspects (a) its organisation for participation rather than imposition, (b) its monitoring procedures for the celebration of learning rather than incessant and stultifying testing, and (c) in its adoption of the more natural Catalogue Curriculum approach.

Therefore, we already have a learning institution in our midst fit for a democracy because it is based on the above principles. It is called the public library system:

> *"There is not such a cradle of democracy upon the Earth as the Free Public Library, this republic of letters where neither rank, office or wealth receives the slightest consideration."*

(Andrew Carnegie)

There are other democratic learning systems, such as museums, nursery centres, home-based education co-operatives (such as *The Otherwise Club*, London and *The Learning Zone*, Isle of Wight) and also Community Arts programmes. So we already know how to make such systems work.

Recently, there was surprise that Finland topped the league tables for school performance despite children starting school much later and having a more learner-friendly school system than countries like England. Public libraries seem to have something to do with it. The country's diverse network of libraries receives the largest single state grant, and new media also encourages reading with many foreign language television programmes. Tomi Kontio, 'the Finns' answer to JK Rowling', explained:

> *"Finns love libraries and our system is probably the best in the world. Every village and suburb has one. I spent almost a third of my childhood in libraries and am happy to pay more taxes to preserve them."*

(from *Times Educational Supplement* 3rd Oct 2003)

Here are some ideas from Bill Ellis of www.*Creating LearningCommunities.org*. He writes that there is currently no perfect library that he knows of, but that it provides a model on which we can build. Could we envisage a learning centre that served all the needs of the self-learner? In addition to books, it might include:

- equipment loans (microscopes, plastic models, telescopes ...),
- a library of learning CDs so that learners could work up the ladder in any topic they choose, when they choose, and how they choose,
- class and meeting rooms so that self-learners could meet regularly and could hire teachers if they wanted,

- a data-base of learning opportunities both in the local community and world-wide including farms, organic farms, factories and museums,
- Community Mentors who have the skills to advise self-learners who want advice.

So, why not phase out schools altogether and ...

"Hand over all school buildings and staff to the Public Library Service, with the brief to augment their existing invitational reading and information services, to develop a comprehensive service of classes, courses and learning experiences in local community centres for personalised learning, responding to the requests and needs of the learners of all ages. The approach of the Public Library Service, after all, is already the customised one, which is why it is our most popular learning institution."

(Roland Meighan in *Times Educational Supplement* 21st June 2002)

John Taylor Gatto, *in The Underground History of American Education,* forecasts a bright future:

"If we closed all government schools, spent twenty times as much as we do on free libraries ... we would quickly find that the American school nightmare had vanished."

We need to add ... and the school nightmare of all the other countries, too.

Derrick Buttress gives us a clear picture of the contrast between the authoritarian approach of school and the autonomous style of the public library in this extract where he gives an account of his own childhood experience, for when in school he was 'in chains', while at the public library he was liberated:

School was boring, but there was no escape from it ... I had an appetite for reading which was unsatisfied by the starvation rations offered by the Junior School's tired text books and the fragments of imaginative literature used by our teachers for purposes other than feeding the imagination. At home, reading was considered a way of passing the time, adding a bit of interest to doing nothing. Usually it was considered an activity for the idle, an excuse for skiving. There were one or two books in the house, occasionally pulp thrillers that Cousin Arthur had given me. Mam and Aunt Mabel read, sometimes, but only the weekly romance papers which they called 'books'. *Lucky Star* and *Red Letter* were their favourites, and I read them too, simply because there was nothing else. They featured short stories with titles such as *Bad Girl* and *He Did Her Wrong,* usually about an honest working-class girl who was made pregnant by some swine with a sports car and bags of money. Men were either shallow lotharios, or honest but lumpen working lads, who always made the best husbands. There was often a drawing of the wronged heroine walking down the terraced street with her head down in shame while older women whispered about her with sneering disapproval of her 'sin' as they stood, their arms folded, on their doorsteps. I read such stories, although they provided little that engaged the imagination, and were not as interesting as the 'true' stories in the *Daily Herald* and the *Evening Post*.

Relief for my word starvation arrived casually, accidently, the consequences of which were to alter the course of my life, although I could understand that only in hindsight many years later. I was on a bus travelling to Aspley, our neighbouring council estate, when Fountain Pen slumped into the seat beside me. He was carrying two hard-backed books with red leatherette covers. He told me he was on his way to Aspley Public Library to change them.
"How much does it cost?" I asked.
"Nothing. You can borrow them for free. I change them every Saturday. My mam doesn't let me go out much, so I read a lot."
That was no surprise. He was, after all, the brainiest lad in the school.
"How do you get in the library?" I asked, wondering if you had to pass an intelligence test.
"Anybody can join. It's easy," he informed me. "You just go in and tell the woman at the desk that you want to join."

Returning from my errand I dropped off the bus at the library, hung outside the glass doors for a few minutes, peeping inside whenever anybody went in, trying to pluck up the nerve to enter and speak to the posh-looking woman at the desk. Eventually I crept in and asked the woman if I could join.

"You'll have to take this card home for your mother to sign. When you bring it back you can borrow two books, but you must bring them back within two weeks. You can have a look round first," she added, and smiled. "The Junior Library is through that door."

I entered the room and felt like yelling in joy. I had never seen so many books in one place, and all for children. Even the smell was beguiling. It would take me for ever to read them all, and the prospect was wonderful. The room was brightly lit and furnished with round tables varnished the colour of honey. Around them there were child-sized chairs with upholstered seats - sheer luxury! Against a wall stood a peculiar wooden projection which looked like the skeleton of an enormous fan. From it hung copies of *The Children's Newspaper*, but they seemed dull reading. A low cabinet was packed with encyclopaedias which seemed to contain everything there was to know in the world, but that wasn't what I wanted to read. High shelving against the walls was divided into sections: History, Hobbies and Games, Nature, Other Lands and Science. But covering at least half of the walls was Fiction - case after case of it from the floor to the high windows. This was exactly what I was looking for.

When I returned about an hour later with my card signed by Mam, I made straight for the fiction shelves. There was so much of it, and so tantalising was the choice, that I didn't know where to look first. A boy wearing the flash blazer and badge of the High Pavement Grammar School strolled in while I gazed up in bewilderment at the walls of fiction. He sauntered around the library with a casual ease that I envied.

"Hiya!" he said cheerily. "Found anything good?"

"I'm just looking," I mumbled, feeling like a trespasser.

"You brought any William books back?"

"No," I said, thinking he at least shared my interest in William the Conqueror - probably a requirement for a grammar school boy.

"Do you like William books?" he asked.

"They're okay. We've done him at our school. I like stories, though."

"William books are stories," he said, not put out by my ignorance.

"About this mad boy called William. They're really wizard."

He strolled across to the 'C' section of the shelves, searched for a moment, pulled out a book and brought it over to me. "Try this," he said. I read the title on the spine: *William the Rebel*. The author was a bloke called Richmal Crompton (later found to be a female).

I began to read it at the bus stop. Then I read it on the bus. I read it as I walked down Frinton Road and carried on reading it when I reached home. Now I was in a world populated by comic boys fighting a never ending battle with potty adults and getting into the kind of scrapes that would have earned me a clout from Mam, but which William Brown got away with. His worst punishment was to spend an early night in the awesome luxury of a room to himself. The plotted daftness made me giggle to myself. I persevered in my reading through the gossip of Mam and Aunt Mabel, through their complaints that I was under their feet and through the chirpy play of Peter and Michael who climbed all over me to divert my attention from the book. But they couldn't. I went to bed that night thankful that my word starvation was behind me. I read until Mam switched the light off in the bedroom because I was wasting the penny in the meter. The Aspley Public Library was the door through which I could escape allowing nothing and no-one to touch me - neither Mam, Aunt Mabel, Dad, Mr. Alkman and Mr. Richards nor the schoolboard man.

There were other discoveries to be made in this unexpected treasure of free reading matter. One surprising fact was that Richmal

Crompton was a woman. How could a woman know so much about kids like William? She was certainly much smarter than Mam and Mabel, and a million times smarter than teachers like Mrs Daft at school. But the world William lived in was a lot different to mine. Maids opened doors, cooks made lunch, which was really dinner, parents had dinner parties and soirees, whatever they were, wearing bow ties and long frocks. School wasn't mentioned much, and then only when William was in trouble there. William and his gang even had their own hut for meetings, and the sun was usually shining on their carefree world. I was drawn to William's world because of its difference from mine just as I was drawn to William because he was relentlessly inventive, bold, and resisted all attempts to civilize him. I was drawn, too, into the world of public school stories because they played out in their own elite way the battle between adult rule and the anarchic free spirit of boys. I ignored the snobbery as the norm in stories - stories were written by the posh so why worry that they were set in a posh world and spoke in a posh accent, unless the character was a handyman or gardener - then he spoke common because he wasn't very bright. I enjoyed the fun, though I would never be able to open my mouth to speak in my common accent if I met somebody from that world of *Topping Towers*.

In contrast I read strange disturbing stories by the Grimm Brothers, tales which I visualised as movies from the Disney studio, and in the style of the scene from Snow White when the beautiful but evil Queen transforms herself into an ugly witch. I wrapped the covers of the library book in brown paper to conceal the evidence from my pals that I was reading 'fairy stories'. I read whatever took my fancy with no direction or interference. I read to suit my mood, and that could lead me to a Biggles adventure, which I thought were rather boring, or to the potted biographies of imperialist heroes such as Wolfe of Quebec and Clive of India. I read and re-read, lovingly, Kipling's *Jungle Book* and *Just So Stories* then skimmed with faint contempt through cruder stories set in the British Empire which related the doing and daring of stiffly moral Englishmen in battle against blacks, Indians and Polynesians. These English gentlemen soldiers and adventurers fought against the odds with guns and cutlasses because the revolting natives were too ignorant to accept civilisation when they had the chance. The quality of the writing mattered to me, although I couldn't have explained why. Some novels were hard to read because they were written in a complicated syntax. Sometimes I gave up if the language and syntax were beyond me. As I gained in experience I discovered that difficulty can provide its own reward. There was a sense of achievement waiting if I got to the end of a challenging book, even if I had not entirely mastered it. Once at the end of a read that had demanded all my concentration I felt that I had made the book my own. In this way I struggled through Dickens's *Tale of Two Cities*, *A Christmas Carol* and *Oliver Twist* as well as Jack London's *White*

Fang and Stevenson's *Treasure Island* like a climber who risks his neck knowing that his effort will reward him with a glimpse of the landscape on top of the cliff, a country of the mind and imagination that only he, of all the people he knows, will be aware of. Mr Alkman and Mr. Richards would have approved of this serious reading had they known about it, although I don't remember ever being encouraged to read in their school, except by Fountain Pen, and outside of school by Cousin Arthur. Perhaps Mr Alkman might have thought my choice of reading matter too eclectic as well as too insular an activity. Was reading alone, especially about the comic activities of William Brown, conducive to learning how to be a Good Citizen? Mr. Richards might well have asked me if such verbal gluttony improved my poor retention of the multiplication tables which I sing-songed every morning on their passage through my numbed brain and into oblivion.

The only immediate measurable effect my visits to the library had on my school career was to make me top of the class in the regular reading tests. It was a phenomenon which seemed to surprise Mrs Daft, who carried them out, and upset the long established order of merit, placing me above a resentful Fountain Pen. He was unaware that he was partially responsible for his own downfall, the innocent instigator of my first tentative moves towards a haphazard self-education.

(from Derrick Buttress, *Broxtowe Boy*, Chapter 12,
Nottingham: Shoestring Press, 2004)

Case Study:

Notschool.net

Notschool.net is a research project run by Ultralab at Anglia Polytechnic University under the watchful eye of Professor Stephen Hepple. It began in the year 2000 and the director is Jean Johnson.

It devises ways of re-engaging young people in education when all else has failed and there is a broad mix of teenagers currently taking part. There are young people excluded from school, sick children, school phobics, young mothers – a range of people that conventional schooling has failed to inspire or cope with.

Others involved include;

Researchers - the name given to the young people in the project; their needs determine any content to be devised.

Tutors – they provide the researchers with learning support as needed.

Mentors – undergraduates or postgraduates who are paid online buddies to a group of researchers.

Governors – high profile people from any walk of life whose role is to provide models of success to encourage the researchers.

Curriculum experts – who are brought in when necessary to create online materials.

In the project, young people learn at their own pace and at a time that suits them. The starting point is to find what interests them and to focus on it, whatever it may be. They become part of a secure on-line learning community that is supportive and has an ethos of self-respect. There is no destructive criticism or blame culture. The young people grow to be proud to show their work and to share their experiences. They manage their own learning with whatever help they require being made available.

Many of the young people turn out to be high achievers within their chosen field of study. The broad and balanced curriculum idea has stifled their progress in the past and they will happily spend hours on a subject that interests them, whether it is art, music, mathematics, ICT or any other focus. Most seem quite capable of making choices about their education and are quite clear about the reasons they have difficulty with schools.

The reports from Notschool.net explain that, given the opportunity to choose their pathway in education, almost all of the young people achieve. The outcomes make it difficult to remember that we are referring to a group of people previously so disengaged from learning that Notschool.net was the last resort. Over 50% have achieved formal qualifications. Over 30% have asked to stay on. Some are now at college, others have their sights on university – a path seemingly closed to them in the past.

It seems clear that these young people needed an alternative to school in order to achieve, and that given this, they can be high achievers. The comments of the young people echo this conclusion: *"It's a shame that kids have to go to the edge before they get on a programme like Notschool.net or into a special unit."* Don Glines of the Education Futures Projects, USA makes a similar point when he declares that to get to the good learning systems in the USA, you first have to be bad at the bad ones.

Bullying is a significant factor since 70% of those taking part in the project report that they were bullied by their peers in school and many of these felt bullied by the teachers as well. The figures may well be higher since this information is not deliberately sought by the project but volunteered in feedback.

The numbers of young people who opt out of the mass schooling system in the UK is currently estimated at 100,000 but the figures could easily be much higher. This figure does not include the 90,000 or more who are fortunate enough to be educated at home. Once young people reject schooling, their options are few.

As noted before, the members of the project are not called pupils, or students, or even clients, (or even curriculum study units, CSUs, as the civil servants who designed the second National Curriculum of 1988 once proposed), but are called 'reseachers'. It is a significant piece of 'rebranding' that signals their switch to a form of autonomous learning.

Sources:
Notschool.net by Jean Johnson in *Education Now News and Review* 36, Summer 2002
Evaluation of the Notschool.net research project Initial Pilot by Julia Duckworth
Notschool.net Research Phase Final Report Dec 2001

Chapter four:

Democratic learning systems

In **democratic education**, the learners as a group have the power to make some, most, or even all of the key decisions, since power is shared and not appropriated in advance by a minority of one or more. In many 'democratic' countries, such educational practices are rare and often meet with sustained, hostile and irrational opposition. Its slogan is usually summed up in the words:

"We did it our way."

Discipline
is democratic discipline by working co-operatively to agreed rules and principles, rather than those imposed by the coercive principle of 'you will do it our way'.

Knowledge
is essentially the skills and information needed by the group to maintain and develop its learning.

Learning
is activity agreed by the group to gain experience, information or particular skills working either together or reporting-back tasks which had been delegated to individuals.

Teaching
is any activity, including formal instruction, that the group judges will lead to effective learning.

Parents
are seen as part of the resources available and potentially as partners in the learning group.

Resources
are anything appropriate to the group's research and learning including people, places, and experiences.

Location
is anywhere that the learning group can meet to pursue effective learning.

Organisation
is commonly in self-regulated groups where dialogue and co-operative learning can take place.

Assessment
is by any form of assessment using any tests, devised by the learners or by others, that are seen to be appropriate to the situation.

Aims
are, essentially, to produce people with the confidence and skills to manage their own life-long learning within a democratic culture.

Power
is shared in the group which is seen as responsible both individually and collectively for its exercise.

Leadership
is shared and revolves, rather than resides in one assertive person. It is expressed in the words of the ancient Chinese sage, Lao-tse:

> *"Of a good leader, they say, when his work is done, we did this ourselves!"*

Some of the consequences of democratic practices that have been found in the research are:

(a) that there is likely to develop a sense of community amongst a group of learners;
(b) there develops a working partnership between appointed teachers and learners;
(c) appointed teachers develop trust in the capability and creative ability of their fellow humans who come to them in the role of students;
(d) dialogue becomes an essential activity rather than an optional feature, and unmandated or imposed learning is not seen as legitimate;
(e) standards of formal work rise, with bonus skills such as increased personal confidence, higher self-esteem, and enhanced discussion and research skills.

Case Study:

A Democratic Learning Co-operative in Teacher Education

Teacher education has been part of a cycle whereby authoritarian classrooms pass students on to authoritarian teacher courses, which produce authoritarian teachers who go back into schools, to sustain and perpetuate authoritarian classrooms, round and round in a closed circle. Breaking out of this cycle is not easy, even when it is seen as desirable. But if it is not broken at the learner-teacher point, teachers go into their careers with no vision of alternatives and no experience of democratic learning. It is usually more difficult to change later.

So, what happened when we tried a democratic approach on a teacher education course? After a short settling-in period, when the students had introduced each other to the group, the news was broken by the tutors, Clive Harber and Roland Meighan, that although there was a planned course ready in the familiar authoritarian expert style, there were other options open to the group. They could consider operating as a democratic learning co-operative which would devise and plan its own programme of studies using the tutors as resources if and when deemed appropriate. A specimen contract was available for discussion purposes if this option required any elaboration.

Specimen group learning contract

- We agree to accept responsibility for our course as a group.

- We agree to take an active part in the learning of the group.

- We agree to be critical, constructively, of our own and other people's ideas.

- We agree to plan our own programme of studies, implement it using the group members and appointed teachers as resources, and review the outcomes in order that we may learn from any limitations we identify.

- We agree to the keeping of a group log-book of work completed, planning decisions, session papers and any other appropriate documents.

- We agree to share the duties of being in the chair, being meeting secretary, session organisers and contributors.

- We agree to review this contract from time to time.

The course thus began as a consultation about the approach to be adopted for the course itself. There was, in fact, another option made available to the group and that was of a mixture of approaches, e.g. adopting one approach for one term and another for another term, or some members choosing an individualised course if the majority wanted either a lecturer-taught course or a learning co-operative.

There is a need to clarify what 'a course' actually meant. In one case it referred to the 'methods of teaching' module of the Post Graduate Certificate of Education year, taking up about one third of the total time. During the period 1976 to 1990, considerable experience of this approach was accumulated as thirteen courses approached their learning in the democratic mode. One course decided to begin with the authoritarian mode and change to the democratic when they felt appropriate. This took about four weeks. This particular course was evaluated by an independent observer and an account published (Fielding et al., 1979).

In two cases, part of the course was run democratically, in one case one day a week, in another for the summer term. The majority of members of these two groups expressed regret in the end of course evaluations that they had not chosen to do the whole of their course as a learning co-operative.

The tutors had to adjust to a different theory of teaching and so did most of the students. All were agreed, however, that the effort was well worthwhile. The new habits were a great improvement on the old ones.

Rationale for a democratic approach

If teaching in secondary schools in the UK is seen primarily as a decision-making activity, one appropriate way of learning to teach may be simulating the process on the training course itself by selecting the aims, content, methods and evaluation methods for their own group. In effect, teachers in training can experiment on themselves, practising many of the skills they will need for the rest of their careers, in contrast to the authoritarian approach of listening to someone else tell them how to make appropriate decisions. Since currently a central activity in secondary schools is formal instruction, students will practise this activity by taking the role of instructor to their fellow students.

In most teacher training there is a marked contrast between the essentially passive role assigned to students at the training institution and the active role on teaching practice. The adoption of a democratic approach weakens this dichotomy since the students become active in both situations.

The outcomes from the learners' viewpoint

No student involved in the thirteen courses wrote an evaluation regretting the debate over the methods they should adopt for the learning, and none of those who opted for a democratic mode has evaluated the experience negatively. No course chose the individualised option, and one student explains the rejection of this approach:

"We decided upon the democratic working co-operative for the following reasons. To begin with we felt that individual work was too isolated. We all felt that the work we had been engaged upon for our first degree courses had been too competitive and too isolated. Therefore, we all agreed that something else had to be attempted for our year within the faculty."

One course resulted in the consultative mode being adopted as a compromise:

"Members of the group decided to choose Option 2 as the most useful method of learning i.e. a course which begins with tutor direction and then gradually handed over decision making to the group. This was essentially a compromise between individuals who wished for a conventional tutor-directed course and those who wanted to try a Democratic Learning Co-operative."

The written evaluations produced by the various group members contained a number of regular themes. One was that of confidence:

"Democratic responsibility, as opposed to sitting back and always receiving, meant that students had to use the skills they already had, as well as learning new ones. Such a situation was a good one in which to develop confidence in one's own thinking."

Most students had something to say about motivation and always in favourable terms:

"I felt great responsibility for the course and this involvement meant always taking a mentally active part. I felt no resentment

against somebody trying to impose work or a situation on me. Thus motivation was high."

"Personally for me the course was very stimulating theoretically and practically. I not only learnt a lot but experienced much. I felt motivated to work and get involved because I felt it was our course."

"There was intellectual enjoyment. Intellectual exploration became an exciting and satisfying end in its own right, rather than a means to a boring and worthless end (e.g. exams, assessment, achieving the teacher's aims, etc.) Ultimately the only end was personal satisfaction, thus the only pressure was personal. Personal pressure stimulated, and made exciting, my learning. Outside pressure always deadened and stifled it."

Several students noted that the discussion techniques of the group members were utilised to the full and developed in the process:

"The discussions were conducted on a relaxed and friendly basis and were therefore enjoyed by most students. Most students felt able to contribute their ideas and opinions to some or all of the topics discussed. Personally I have found this aspect of the course very beneficial because it has facilitated the exchange of ideas and information between group members and the exploration of many different aspects of key issues."

One of the conventional objections to democratic learning is that the content may be deficient if the 'experts' let go of the selection of the 'best' content for the task in hand. The students did not support this interpretation:

"With all students choosing the range of subjects the content, inevitably (in my mind) was of a greater range and more relevance than if the 'teacher' had done all the choosing. A group of students, especially from different specialist backgrounds, were able to provide more resources than one teacher could."

"The standard of papers given was generally very high - probably much higher than if the work had been set by the tutor."

The democratic nature of the course meant that decision making was practised and that responsibility was shared. The students found this a favourable feature of the course:

"Responsibility and authority were dispersed among all members of the group, meaning that the assumption of these was voluntary, rather than them being concentrated into one person's (teacher) job. The taking of responsibility on a voluntary basis did not present any problems as all members of the group were happy to take it."

"A system whereby 'rules' were made, but made by ourselves as we went along, meant that the group had security and direction, but also adaptability and flexibility."

"One was encouraged to recognise the value of other students as a resource."

"The content of the course would be decided by the group. Essentially this meant that the group decided its priorities - what the particular members of the group felt would be most useful to them as future teachers. It allowed members of the group to follow up personal interests and also allowed the group to draw upon the expertise that did exist within the group."

A regular theme that occurred in the student evaluation was that of the bridging of theory and practice. Since a dichotomy is frequently reported between those two, it is interesting to see what the learners in a democratic situation had to say about this matter:

"With regard to the 'methods' course, any gaps between theory and practice were, I think, well bridged. The peculiar nature of the course, with its options (including the more radical democratic learning co-operative) offered and put into practice, meant that we did not just talk about alternative ways of teaching and learning but to a certain, albeit perhaps limited, extent, experienced and experimented with alternative methods."

There was also comment on a related tension between the problems of preparing for survival in schools as they were, whilst considering any vision as to improvements on the status quo or alternatives to the current orthodoxy:

"The course, in practice, therefore, seemed to me to cope nicely with the idealism of educational change and the practicalities and constraints involved in operationalizing such changes. In this way the course provided a realistic 'vision' for changed procedures in teaching while not ignoring the problems of practice, or survival, which face all teachers."

"The experience of a democratic learning co-operative is valuable in itself for intending teachers since it presents them with an alternative method of learning and teaching for future use with their own pupils. Unless this is actually experienced by students, it is unlikely that this important innovation will reach schools in any significant degree."

"One of the roles of teacher training should be to investigate and experiment with alternative methods of teaching and learning, in a practical way, and to provide working models of the alternative methods."

The co-operative outlook to learning which is basic to the democratic approach extended in influence beyond the methods course in the university to the teaching practice situation:

"During the major Teaching Practice and in other instances the co-operative tended to be very supportive and relationships proved to be advantageous, especially during the ten long weeks of teaching practice in the spring term."

Most of the evaluations concluded with an overall verdict on the course:

"The group enjoyed the Methods Course very much. It was extremely beneficial both academically and practically. Highlights and reservations along with possible improvements and alterations were suggested, and a general report on the course was made which had the consent of the whole group."

"I hope other groups will learn from our experiences and enjoy their year as much as I believe our course has."

"The co-operative spent many hours in discussion and formulated opinions and views (often varying) in relation to our timetable of work. All the group members felt without any reservation whatsoever that the co-op was a new working experience which was stimulating, enjoyable and very worthwhile. We all gained an enormous amount from it, academically and in relation to the new relationships we formed. Everyone in the working co-operative agreed that it was an invaluable, exciting experience and one which we would advise any PGCE students to take part in regardless of discipline."

The outcomes from the tutors' point of view

The tutor involved in the first attempts and the second tutor involved later kept personal notes week by week on the democratic learning co-operatives. Some of the themes that are selected from these notes as significant are as follows.

A potential conflict was seen in the transfer from the democratic course to the authoritarian schools in which teaching practice took place. The tutors were surprised at the pay-off from the course, which seemed to more than offset any expected responses of alienation and rejection. The students approached the Teaching Practice with considerable confidence, and this was remarked upon by the teachers in the school. Since the students were used to making decisions about what to learn and how, assembling appropriate materials and using them, they appeared to transfer these behaviours to school scheme and lesson preparation without any nervousness. They were also used to working co-operatively and so fitted into team situations with teachers with relative ease.

Tutor's visits held little fear for them since they were already used to the tutor's presence at their 'performances' at the university. None attempted to implement learning co-operatives, with the exception of one attempt at sixth-form level, which was, reportedly, successful, but all approached pupils in either the 'nice strict' mode or the consultative mode and relationships with classes were remarkably smooth from the outset in most cases.

The tutors had to adjust to a different theory of teaching since they had been educated in authoritarian styles. They had to learn to listen much more, learn to resist the previous habit of dominating the decision-making and discussions, and to cope with anxiety when their expertise was seen to be less significant than they had previously supposed. There was irony in feeling anxious at having helped students to manage competently on their own when this is exactly what they will need to do for the rest of their professional careers. The facilitative role was demanding since making contacts, identifying resources and solving operational problems on the spot or at short notice were different experiences to the authoritarian approach (where, having made the decisions as to content in advance, a tutor was in a position to produce handouts and identify resources some time beforehand). The tutors also had to cope with their ideas and suggestions being either rejected or scrutinised closely and justification requested.

There were tensions with the other courses that the students were required to attend as part of their PGCE year. The confidence of members of the learning co-operative in challenging other tutors in formal lectures was not always welcome, and other students did not always find their enthusiasm and commitment appealing. On one occasion there was a joint session with another methods group to work with a visiting speaker. When she phoned to say she was unable to come due to a school crisis, the learning co-operative immediately set about organising a substitute programme for the morning for themselves. The other student teachers group declined to take part or devise something similar for themselves and went away to take the morning off with some parting remarks about the others being far too keen.

Any anxieties the tutors had about the quality of student input or the 'covering of key topics' proved groundless. The students exceeded what the tutors had planned and added ideas that had not been included, so that the tutors were learning new material in some of the sessions.

The tutors were curious as to how the students would cope with applications for posts and interviews. Potential teachers of social and political studies sometimes have to cope with hysteria about their subject - not unlike that which biology teachers used to face because of their identification with evolution theory in Bible-belt communities - but in addition, this group had a democratic experience that had appeared to increase confidence, commitment and awareness of alternative approaches to education. It seemed a potentially explosive combination. However, the pay-off from the course appeared to be positive rather than negative. The approach of the students seemed to appeal to many interviewers. Some head teachers have responded to the effect that 'this is a whole new generation of teachers, articulate, enthusiastic, industrious and challenging'. Perhaps the tutors should have known better because when they had organised teach-ins with in-service courses using the members of the democratic learning co-operative as a resource, the response of the experienced teachers had frequently been similarly enthusiastic.

Conclusion

If democratic ideologies of education have in common a view of independence in the teacher-learner relationship, the outcome is a type of power sharing and an exercise in freedom in the sense that Wright Mills (1959) expounded:

"Freedom is, first of all, the chance to formulate the available choices, to argue over them and then the opportunity to choose. That is why freedom cannot exist without an enlarged role of human reason in human affairs."

The democratic learning co-operatives approach appears to exemplify this principle and also allow a bridging back into the authoritarian situations of schools with positive effects, so that the student teachers appeared to be well prepared to cope with schools as they are, but also having experiences and visions of possible alternatives and possible modifications to the status quo should the situation allow or require them.

Case study:

Democratic practices in schools

The following reports are from people who have experienced democratic practices in education. For Sonia Bonner, her A Level Sociology course left a lasting impression. James Baldaro, a student on one of these A Level courses, is now training to be a teacher. Lesley Browne encountered democratic learning methods on her initial teacher training course for her Post Graduate Certificate of Education. She subsequently offered her students the chance to experience the same process.

Reflections of a secondary school student

Sonia Bonner reports:

"Although my memories of sixth form are fading fast, the one thing still highlighted for me is the Sociology Democratic Learning Co-operative. After twelve years of 'traditional' learning and soaking up the information I was fed, it was a most refreshing change to be given a choice.

"On starting A Level Sociology I was pleasantly surprised by the democratic attitude taken towards our course. At first many of us were unsure about taking on so much responsibility for our education, what with the extra pressure of just beginning A Levels. Also the thought of putting our learning in the hands of our class mates, no matter how much we liked them, was a bit daunting. However, it soon came to light that the idea appealed to our academic curiosity and after much debate we all agreed to give it our best shot.

"It took a great deal of deliberation before the contract was signed by everyone, as we all thought it too important to rush. Some obvious clauses were introduced into the contract at the beginning. For example, we must share work for mutual benefit which was the whole backbone of the DLC. Also every lesson should be attended and deadlines should be met and essays completed. Later, we added into the contract that someone should chair each lesson.

"Furthermore, the fact that we were taking responsibility as a group was of paramount importance. This gave us a collective concern for our learning and a strong group bonding. We agreed to evaluate our progress at the end of every term, so we were all able to express our thoughts and air any problems. We also understood throughout the contract that our teachers were to be

used as a resource for the group and were requested to stand in if anyone was off ill. With this in the contract everyone felt as if they had some support and were not totally alone.

"The reasons we had clauses like 'We must be kind, respectful and competent, not right', was to remind everyone of the principles of the Co-operative. So, the contract helped us to form an understanding of our rules and contributed significantly to the DLC's success.

"It soon became apparent that everyone was very dedicated, perhaps because it was a different way of learning or because it was what we had wanted all along. The bonding of the group was very strong straight away and the first lessons were full of enthusiasm. I remember being entertained by quizzes, cartoon drawings, new and topical material, including current affairs. All of these new stimulants made the whole learning experience very enjoyable and, more importantly, effective.

"The success of the Co-operative was also shown through its failures! For example, when lessons didn't go according to plan or if the group member who was taking the lesson didn't turn up, then the group reacted very differently than before. We became outraged that a fellow student would let us down like this. However, before experiencing the DLC we would have all been very happy to have gone home for the afternoon if the teacher had failed to turn up. However, for a while when our teacher was ill we continued with the lessons, sticking to the timetable and motivating ourselves.

"I remember when I prepared my own lesson. I took considerable time planning it and was very proud of the work I had done. It was a wonderful feeling teaching your peers, and providing them with quality information. I took as much time over their lesson as I would have expected them to do for me.

"Although we didn't follow the DLC through to our final exam, the time we spent doing it was invaluable. It made me take an active part in my education, helped me understand what a group effort could produce, and how important it is to experiment with teaching methods and not always to be the receiver."

Embarking on teacher training – the views of a former participant in democratic learning, James Baldero:

"I have never let my schooling interfere with my education."

"Mark Twain's quote perhaps best sums up my experiences of education up until the age of sixteen. There I left secondary schooling relatively successful but ultimately disillusioned with the institution of the school and its teacher-dominated learning.

"Upon returning to education a year later to do an A Level Politics course I found such fears and prejudices challenged by my involvement in a democratic learning co-operative. The formal creation of the Co-operative, its structure and implementation, are discussed elsewhere. What I hope to offer here are my recollections. Importantly, I aim to look at how these experiences have helped shape my perceptions and influence my actions throughout university and beyond, as today I myself move towards a career in education.

"In 1981 H.M.I. in Teacher Training and the Secondary School (D.E.S.) commented that:

'There is scope for more small group work which genuinely involves student participation and far less reliance upon the set lecture and tutor dominated seminar'.

"This key notion of 'student participation' was an essential and recurrent theme of our Democratic Learning Co-operative. As students, we were involved in every aspect of the decision-making process. I can remember the surprise of all the group members at being given the power to choose the particular syllabus we were to follow, the actual subjects within the syllabus we were to cover and, most surprisingly of all, the specific teaching methods the course would involve. Any understandable apprehension quickly vanished as we were reassured by the language of the Co-operative: negotiation, tolerance, choice, mutual support and of course democracy. Not just as politics students but as a representative group of sixth formers these key words appealed to us and to our sense that we deserved a certain level of responsibility.

"Within the group each of us took an active role in the creation of a positive classroom atmosphere, something my experience had only ever previously defined in negative terms. As a Co-operative we felt that our role in the initial decision-making process was crucial. Obviously, individuals had little working knowledge of the syllabuses so we recognised at an early stage the benefit of using the teacher as a resource. More importantly though, the group highlighted the fact that individual group members, being equal to the teacher, could also suggest topics and ideas not previously considered.

"Essentially the group was able to construct its own study programme using the resources available. Significantly my one outstanding memory of this time is the overwhelming sense that this was our course. Indeed, after listening back over the interview tapes from 1991, this proved to be the most commonly used phrase. Tina's comments on the initial course choices underline this:

"I think it's really good, but I think more courses should be like this. It's more our course. We are teaching each other ... I'm proud of myself and it's given me more confidence".

"This last point, that of increased confidence amongst group members, leads me to what I believe was the key success of the Democratic Learning Co-operative: the development of transferable skills. Another comment from a group member relates specifically to this:

"Democratic responsibility, as opposed to sitting back and always receiving, means that we have a chance to use existing skills as well as learning new ones."

"It was not until my time in higher education that I began to acknowledge such skills and trace them back to my democratic learning experience. Perhaps the most obvious of these transferable skills was seminar work. Seminars were not so overwhelming for me, as I felt, to some extent, that I had experienced the possibilities and problems of communication and confidence through the DLC. Moreover, in negotiating course choices and in advising and supporting other group members we had developed key political skills. These, too, were useful at university and appear essential to any career in education!

"Obviously such a radical change in approach to our studies did present some early problems. These were rarely of a truly negative nature and the established group structure was successful in offering reassurance and encouragement. To me at the time and still today, I believe that the creation of this group culture is essential for any school wishing to offer a positive learning experience away from the long established care and support structures of the school and sixth form. The Co-operative represented a kind of inner circle that quickly began to tackle the kind of minor problems of confidence and motivation within the group that are so often the principal worries of sixth form students.

As Nicole commented:

"Everyone did a little bit, we all help each other. If I hadn't done my part, other people would have suffered. I felt responsible for them."

"I feel that this point was particularly significant with relevance to the age of the group members. Being 16-18 we were seeking to redefine our pupil/school relationship. A common complaint throughout sixth forms is 'stop treating us like kids!'. The DLC offered us not only a different pupil/teacher relationship, but perhaps more importantly, it rewarded us with a quintessential responsibility for our own learning, development and destiny.

"The relative success of the group in external examination results, despite seeming to mean 'everything' at the time is actually secondary. The real success of the Democratic Learning Co-operative lies in how it instilled key notions of co-operation, mutual support and tolerance in a group of 16-18 year olds. These are skills which reach far beyond the short-term goals of A Level examinations and university graduation. Coupled with the confidence developed through the DLC's reliance on continued public speech, teaching and discussion with others, I believe our experiences equipped us with essential transferable skills. In my own case it was an experience which has ironically helped to change and shape my own perceptions and expectations of teaching as I embark on a career in education."

Democratic Learning in a secondary school – teacher Leslie Browne's experience

"Democratic approaches to learning are a rarity in the British education system. However, in 1985 I was given the opportunity to participate in a democratic learning environment on a teacher training course run by Roland Meighan and Clive Harber. This experience provided the most positive and satisfying educational experience I have ever encountered. I found the process so worthwhile that for the last five years Advanced Level Sociology and Politics students at the school where I teach have similarly been given the opportunity to choose how they learn.

"The courses begin with an initial discussion and presentation which looks at different methods of learning. The choices include the conventional teacher-directed course, a teacher-based consultative model, a democratic learning co-operative and an individualised course of the Open University type. The teacher

also suggests that a mixture of these options is possible to allow for some individual preferences.

"The aim of setting up a democratic learning environment is to enable young people to take responsibility for their own learning. This means that they decide their own agenda, then they work individually or in small groups preparing lessons, making visits, planning and leading presentations, organising visiting speakers and so on. Other aims are to increase students' self-reliance, to increase confidence, to develop skills of articulation and investigation, and to remove the myth that the teacher is expert in all things.

"The initial discussion is an exercise in the important skill of group decision-making. After much debate the 1989/91 A Level group - and more recently the 1992/4 group - decided on the democratic model of learning. Whenever this choice is made, it is important to create a classroom atmosphere that promotes the values of tolerance, fairness, and openness to change. These encourage student contributions and participation.

"At the pre-democratic stage the students are given a specimen democratic learning contract. This consists of a written contract which lays down the ground rules for the Co-operative. The original contract presented to the students was one devised by Harber and Meighan for the PGCE course in Social and Political Education at The University of Birmingham.

"The process of devising a contract can be a long and at times painful one. The students then go on to choose a syllabus that they wish to follow and the areas they wish to be responsible for. All students take part in a number of presentations which use the full range of teaching and learning styles. In fact, the range is far greater than the teacher would normally use. The final session of each term includes a review of the course.

"Possibly one of the most important practices in democratic learning environments is that of dialogue between students and teachers, questioning and discussing together how they might improve their practice. If democracy in the classroom is about anything, it is the free exchange of ideas. Without this open continuous debate, power-sharing is pointless."

Some of the comments of students on Lesley Browne's courses were as follows:

"Because people know that they have the responsibility of taking lessons they are likely to put a lot of effort into their presentations."

"The democratic way of learning has been very interesting and enjoyable. It has proved that learning can be fun and interesting."

"I think having to do the research for the lessons ourselves is a good way to learn the topic; it improves our research skills and you have to understand it better so you can explain it to others."

"Pupils contribute more in discussions so grow in confidence when talking in groups. Skills such as these may not be used so much if another form of learning was used."

"I used to see you as the 'expert', because of your knowledge of the subject, but now I see you as more of a resource directing us to places."

"It makes you think more, doesn't it, it makes you feel a bit more responsible."

"It was refreshing to be able to choose the syllabus and topics that interested you."

"I have not only learnt a lot but experienced much. I feel motivated to work and get involved because it is our course."

"By setting up a democratic learning environment, power was shared by all members of the group."

Teacher education and breaking the cycle

A key feature of democracy is the principle that those who are affected by a decision have the right to take part in the decision-making. This is expressed in slogans such as *'No taxation without representation!'* If we apply this to schools, we get, *'No learning and therefore no curriculum without the learners having a say in the decision-making'.*

In the usual approach to schooling, however, there is a chronic fear of trusting students and sharing power with them. In the everyday life of schools, we find a fear of opting for the discipline of democracy. Instead, teachers resort to an exclusive diet of hierarchical order and authoritarian discipline. Indeed, as we saw earlier, Carl Rogers in *Freedom to Learn* in the 80s noted that democracy and its values are actually **scorned and despised**:

"Students do not participate in choosing the goals, the curriculum, or the manner of working. These things are chosen for the students. Students have no part in the choice of teaching personnel, nor any voice in educational policy. Likewise the teachers often have no choice in choosing their administrative officers ... All this is in striking contrast to all the teaching about the virtues of democracy, the importance of the 'free world', and the like. The political practices of the school stand in the most striking contrast to what is taught. While being taught that freedom and responsibility are the glorious features of our democracy, students are experiencing powerlessness, and are having almost no opportunity to exercise choice or carry responsibility."

A few schools throughout the world have introduced elements of democratic practice into their basic authoritarian framework. Summerhill, UK is a well known residential one where A.S.Neill established the general running of the school by the school 'moot', but this always excluded the curriculum. Attendance of classes was voluntary, and the lessons were organised and provided by the teachers (see www.summerhill.co.uk). Sands School is a day school in the UK run on similar lines, (see sandschool.demon.co.uk). and so is Wolverhampton Grammar School. (See Trafford, B. 1997.)

Sudbury Valley, USA goes further and puts the curriculum in the hands of the students. There is no timetable until the students devise one. As the students devise classes, workshops and courses, sometimes using the paid members of staff, and sometimes not, a thriving and well-ordered programme of studies emerges. (See www.sudval.org)

Case study:

Home-based educating families in co-operation:
The Otherwise Club

The *Otherwise Club's* roots go back to 1990, to the home of a family, the Barsons, with a long-term vision of providing a community centre for home educators. The group quickly expanded beyond the capacity of a family home, and in February 1993 new premises were found in Kilburn, London. It was here that *The Otherwise Club* began in its present form. Currently there are in the region of forty families with each family paying membership fees towards the cost of renting premises, regular workshops, educational visits and holidays together.

Leslie Barson gives three rules of thumb that she has learnt from the last ten years at club. The first rule of thumb is to be eternally patient. Children take adults' censure to heart. You may not mean to be hurtful but a young person can feel it that way. Please, always (and we are all human) try to take a breath before saying something negative to a child or young person.

The second rule is to be ever flexible. You may decide to do X craft. When the children arrive they do Y activity with your ideas and craft materials. Often, if you are truthful, their ideas are better than yours were. And even if the children's activity is not actually better, it is truly better because it comes from the people who are supposed to be benefiting from the activity. If you want to do X craft do it for yourself. Do not try to justify making others do it by saying it is good for them. In fact a further ramification of this rule of thumb is *"Always beware of anyone telling you to do something 'for your own good'"*. The last rule of thumb, I am afraid is self-explanatory and practical. Never turn down money!

The Barson family thanks all those who have supported the club enthusiastically through thick and thin over the past ten years. It is this sort of support for the club in particular but for home-based education in general that is invaluable and enables projects like theirs to thrive. They are very excited and proud that this project in alternative education has touched so many people's lives over the past ten years. The *Otherwise Club* remains a unique project in alternative education and looks forward to its continuation.

Chapter five:

Interactionist learning systems

In the **interactive approach to education**, the authoritarian, democratic and autonomous ideologies are used in a variety of patterns. They may be alternated, or revolved or used in some order of ranking. Its slogan is usually summed up in the words:

"We did it in a variety of ways."

It looks like a simple solution – just take bits from the three basic learning systems and get the benefits of all three. I have made out a case along these lines in the past as regards the problem of discipline. I have argued that there is a crucial difference between various forms of order, sometimes known as discipline systems or the 'problem of discipline' as it is commonly referred to in discussions about education. One difference is between that of authoritarian order and authority on the one hand, and democratic order and authority on the other. There is also the third approach of autonomous order and authority where individuals exercise self-discipline.

When my son was four-years-old, he reprimanded me for kicking our plastic ball on to a rosebush. We were playing football at the time. He was quite right because we had agreed the rule that this was not the thing to do, since it could puncture the thin skin of the ball. I accepted his reprimand. Quietly, I did claim extenuating circumstances - that it had been accidental and not a deliberate act. My father, who witnessed the incident, was horrified. Later he accused me of 'corrupting the child by weakening my authority as an adult'. He was one of those people who had come to the conclusion that discipline is the simple problem of adults making children behave to instructions.

This is only one kind of discipline - the authoritarian. As we saw earlier, three kinds can be identified.
(i). **Authoritarian** - where order is based on rules imposed by adults. Power resides in an individual or group of leaders. Its slogan is: *'You will do it my (or the management's) way!'*
(ii). **Autonomous** - where order is based on self-discipline and self-imposed rational rules. Power resides with the individual. Its slogan is: *'I did it my way.'*

(iii). **Democratic** - where order is based on rules agreed after rational discussion i.e. based on evidence, human rights values and the logic of consequences. Power is shared amongst the people in the situation. Its slogan is: *'We did it our way.'*

There has been a centuries-old debate about which of these three is the best system of discipline. It is now a sterile debate. The complexities of modern life are such that **all three types of discipline** have a part to play in the scheme of things. Sometimes we need to follow instructions, or take on leadership roles, thus following the authoritarian approach. Therefore, in an aeroplane, debating who should fly the aircraft and the rules of flying is not the appropriate form of discipline that matches the situation. In a car, however, drivers need autonomous discipline and to make the decisions about driving the car without the confusions of being over-ruled by an authoritarian or advised by a committee of back-seat drivers.

In many other situations, such as running a 'convivial' rather than a 'coercive' school, many heads are likely to be better than one in deciding the rules to be adopted, based on the evidence and the rights of all involved. This is democratic power-sharing, and although it can be time-consuming at first, it leads to better, fairer, and accepted decisions with a co-operative system of order.

There are three types of error as regards the question of discipline. One, the current error of most UK schooling, is to select the authoritarian as the exclusive or predominant approach. The second, the error of some radical thinkers, is to make the autonomous the 'One Right Way'. The third error, from another radical tradition, is to make the democratic the exclusive approach. All these 'One Right Way' approaches fail to match the need for young people to learn what most of their elders have clearly failed to learn, that is, how to be competent in the logistics and practice of all three types of discipline, and to select them appropriately.

A fourth error is to regard all three as of equal status and allocate equal time to them. In the modern world, the democratic form of discipline is, in the end the most significant, firstly, on the grounds that Winston Churchill proposed - that democracy is the worst form of organisation - **except for all the alternatives.** It follows, that if you do not have democratic discipline controlling the others, you will inevitably have something worse such as tyranny, domination, bureaucracy, or bullying authoritarianism.

In contrast, 'One Right Way' approaches have a strong tendency to 'play cuckoo' and heave the eggs of the others out of the nest. The error of some radical educators was to allow no place at all for the authoritarian approach. Apart from the need for 'discipline flexibility' in the modern world, authoritarian control is sometimes necessary to protect children, but always, as Bertrand Russell proposed, **in the spirit of freedom**. This means that it is a temporary expedient only, until one of the other forms of discipline can take over. Explaining the reasons to children is then essential as a prelude to agreeing rules and reasons. 'For your own good' and 'because I say so', the stock in trade assertions of so many authoritarians, are not good enough reasons in themselves.

The sad conclusion is that most schools in the UK, by ignoring the democratic form of discipline, are doing their pupils a grave disservice. The result, Chris Shute argues in his book *Compulsory Schooling Disease*, is that **the obsessive use of authoritarian imposed discipline is the actual cause of many of the social problems it sets out to 'cure'**. Such schools have been involved since the start, in compulsory mis-education.

The problem of the default position

As regards whole learning systems, however, there is a crucial question of the default position. Does the system default to authoritarian or the autonomous or the democratic definitions? In the 1960s and 1970s the basic position of the learning system called mass schooling was authoritarian but some cautious moves had begun to be made in the direction of democratic and also autonomous options. Such moves angered those in our society with strong totalitarian tendencies in their mentality. At the same time that I was writing about the somewhat limited and timid nature of these moves, others were portraying them hysterically as laissez-faire, 'anything goes' and license to run riot. Some schools, the secondary school Risinghill and the primary school William Tyndale, were singled out for scrutiny and relentless negative interpretation often based on exaggerated or invented stories.

A campaign in England entitled the *Campaign for Real Education* was, in reality, a campaign for Real Authoritarian Schooling, asserted dogmatically as the One Right 'Common-Sense' Way for everybody to learn. Evidence for this position is dubious so insults are used to fill the gaps. A particular target is 'progressive education' and the opposite of this would appear to be 'regressive education' which is said to be superior:

*"Advocates of regressive education have resorted to labelling anyone who agreed with them as a sensible person and anyone who disagreed with them in insulting terms. In one booklet alone, **What Is Wrong With Our Schools,** anyone who took a opposing view to that being offered was described as crazy, or brainwashed, or flashy, or new-style, or faceless facilitators, or Politically Motivated Intruders, or progressives, or child-centred activists, or wets, or hotheads, or loonies, or nihilists. The writers contributing to this book were liable to contradict each other on fundamental issues and so run the risk of having to insult each other."*
(Meighan (1993) p.7. *Theory and Practice of Regressive Education*)

Since there was no real crisis, (though there was a need to carry on improving as fast as possible), the media worked on it until there was one established in the national consciousness. Even the venerable *Readers' Digest* joined with an emotive article entitled, *These Teachers Teach Trouble* which ended up with an official complaints enquiry about its sources. The notorious Black Papers added to the manufacture of a crisis atmosphere.

The outcome was the Education Act of 1988 which took the system back one hundred years to the default position of the extreme authoritarian package based on a rigid National Curriculum, incessant testing and aggressive inspection. A previous chief inspector of schools, Edmond Holmes, who had tried to make such a system work for thirty years, wrote two books, *What Is and What Might Be* published in 1911 and *The Tragedy of Education* published in 1921, stating his shame at having been a party to it.

In contrast, the democratic learning system can be designated as the default position. It can incorporate features of the other two systems as it develops. To illustrate this point, when I was involved with young teachers in training using the democratic approach, the group planned, administered and evaluated their own programme of learning. The paid tutors acted as learning coaches. The group would delegate considerable amounts of the preparatory work to be done autonomously by individuals. In deciding the best way to learn a particular theme or skill, the group would sometimes choose to submit to an authoritarian form of learning by inviting a speaker, who was usually interviewed by designated group members rather than given a free hand, as appropriate for that particular task.

Teachers have proved that the democratic approach is effective with all ages of children. Head teacher Bernard Trafford in his book *Participation, Power-sharing and School Improvement* shows how this is working in Wolverhampton Grammar School. John Ingram and Norman Worrall in their *Teacher-Child Partnership: the negotiated classroom* show how this works with infant and junior classes. Families, whether home-schooling or not, who discuss, negotiate, and share decision-making, also engage in democratic discipline.

It is also possible to have the autonomous learning system as the default position, and in an important sense this is what many home-based educators do when they reject the present schooling system and opt for learner-managed learning instead. They may then work in democratic learning co-operatives with other families at times or opt back into the school system for a time, but always they can revert to the autonomous home-based system if these variations fail to work well enough.

Case study:

Mankato Wilson School, USA

As described by Don Glines who took over the existing school of 600 students and its staff, and introduced 69 changes simultaneously. It was transformed from a standard authoritarian school into an interactive mode with strong elements of autonomy and democracy, resulting in a vibrant learner-friendly place.

The 'new' Wilson was created overnight. Prior to the change, the 'old' Wilson operated as a good conventional campus laboratory school with the usual waiting list. There was little choice for the students. Within one month of the decision to create the most experimental, year-round alternatives programme in America, the total 'revolution' was under way. Completely dismantling tradition with an existing staff, Wilson became a 'model' illustrating the tremendous potential for changing outmoded schooling at a rapid, dramatic pace, while additionally challenging conventional thinking, and offering visions of continuing innovation. It caused discussion on the future of learning, while providing a significantly different environment for those who volunteered to participate in the search for a transformation.

Wilson staff made 69 changes immediately. The most important issue was the aspect of human relations. Students selected their own facilitators and advisors; later surveys and interviews determined that consciously and subconsciously, the advisors and teachers were chosen on the basis of six factors: personality, perception, age, gender, interest, and skill. The students found the adult they most trusted and asked that person to serve as their confidante. No one was ever assigned to a teacher or advisor; no teacher was ever assigned to a student. As a result, all courses and requirements were eliminated. Curriculum became what the students wanted to study at the moment in time, with the persons they most wanted to share their learning. Creativity was addressed, as the greatest number of dropouts in many schools are those who score highest on 'creativity tests'. Learning styles were a prime consideration. Students selected staff who were more rigid or more flexible depending upon their relationships and current perceived needs in given areas. The youngest learners had the same choices as seniors; they were offered more assistance by advisors, teachers, older students, aides, and parents, but otherwise were relatively self-directing.

Curriculum was personalised and then individualised. Some four-year-olds were reading at the 2nd grade level; some 2nd graders were not reading and were not in remedial classes. Both maturation and motivation needed the right blends. Five phases of learning opportunities were stressed: (1) individual instruction/discussion, (2) independent study, (3) open labs, (4) small groups (with and without staff), and (5) voluntary common thread large groups.

To facilitate such a programme, Wilson was open year-round. Families of construction workers in the states like Minnesota need to vacation in January, not July; Florida families wanting to snow ski find June-July-August not the best period in the Rockies. Homelessness and low incomes occur all twelve months. Attendance was optional for each day. Food was served all day in the student centre. The student mix in all areas was non-graded. The youngest learners and seniors had the same/similar programmes, philosophies, facilities, instructors, climates, and environments; they were separated only when desired or appropriate. They often shared activities and helped each other learn.

One of the attractions to visitors was how Wilson went from a traditional schedule to a non-scheduled environment - a daily smorgasbord of choices where all students and teachers created different time allotments every day. Personalising the day/year was not hard to accomplish in a school of 600 - or as a school-within-a-school on a large campus - once the curriculum and instruction were individualised and students learned to be self-directing. A major key to the success of Wilson was responsibility; the concept is not taught, but must be given and accepted. The climate belief stated: "with freedom goes responsibility and courtesy. In larger school-within school plans, one choice can allow for the same non-schedule philosophy. There were no report cards, no class rank lists, and no traditional transcripts. Students completed goal sheets with their selected staff. There were no graduation requirements; students left when ready with approval of their advisors, parents, and a review committee, though a great majority received their diplomas after the conventional twelve years. They stayed because they liked it, for financial or home reasons, their age, or involvement with sports and friends; but they could, and many did, graduate earlier, or later, than usual.

The physical environment was changed; walls were cut with arches or removed or constructed. The interior was painted interesting colours and part of the facility was carpeted. The 'Beginning Life Centre' focused on 3, 4, 5, and 6 year-olds who could stay there all or part of the day, but who could also participate throughout the building, which almost all did. Parents returned some evenings.

Both 'special education' and 'gifted' students were completely mainstreamed as early as 1968. Community service and volunteering were critical components. Wilson people were 'everywhere' but were especially involved in the senior citizens home and the state mental hospital as aides, friends and learners. A highlight experience for most students was the Mexican exchange with Centre Escolar in Puebla. Participating Wilson youth spent eight weeks in Mexico, increasing their fluency in Spanish and learning the culture. The Mexican youth reciprocated by coming to Mankato four weeks each year. Lasting relationships were common, as many students and parents continued to exchange visits 20 years after leaving Wilson.

There were no eligibility rules for sports, no sets of textbooks, no rows of desks facing the chalkboard, no bells, no notes from home, no hall passes or study halls - all common in the Midwest in the Wilson era - and certainly no self-contained classrooms. Student teachers and master degree interns learned to 'teach', (meaning to facilitate learning), at Wilson; they could be exempted from all traditional college of education classes and still receive their degrees and credentials. Unlike most alternatives, Wilson maintained competitive sports, (reaching the State finals in basketball), cheerleaders, dance, drama, music, and art.

Personalised Year Calendar

In theory, the site was open 365 days a year, 24 hours each day. In facility and staff reality, it was 240 days, the result of the usual budget restraints. The learning contract followed a basic formula. Students 'owed' the school 170 days. They could attend any 170 of the 240 the facility was open, or all 240, or gain 'credit' through off-campus ventures, such as: volunteering in the community, mountain climbing in Colorado, French in Quebec, Spanish in Puebla, Sioux cultures at Pine Ridge, helping grandparents in senior homes, assisting the homeless, for any of the 365 calendar days, including Christmas. With the curriculum completely personalised and individualised, students and staff had the advantage of almost complete flexibility.

There were no coverage for absence problems, as faculties worked in teams of teachers with whatever combinations of aides, volunteers, community resources, and student interns were available at a given moment. If 600 students were enrolled, it was assumed that perhaps 500 would attend each day, allowing three to five or more teachers to be absent; balance was not a problem. Families, students, and staff could vacation whenever they desired year-round

- for a day, week, a month or more. They did not have to ask permission, but notification was requested for longer periods

Conclusion

Totally new learning systems are truly needed for the coming decades. Wilson adaptations can serve as transition patterns. To make a Wilson 'work,' the philosophy regarding youth and learning is the key. However, the 'mechanics' must be implemented correctly, for a crumbling structure can defeat the concept. Therefore, in general, the programme must embrace with understanding the following components:

- non-gradedness,
- working in teams,
- personalised and individualised curriculum,
- self-selected requirements,
- selection of advisors and teachers by students,
- self-directed assessment,
- responsibility and courtesy,
- continuous programmes,
- volunteering,
- beginning life centres,
- stimulus centres,
- year-round education,
- interdependent learning,
- programme-without-walls,
- family-designed conferences,
- optional attendance,
- open facilities,
- non-textbook approaches,
- everyone eligible, and
- flexible scheduling.

There are 69 or more such changes, but when welded as one, they comprise a humane transition toward new learning systems.

Case Study:

Citischool - a school without walls where young people are citizens and citizens are teachers

Tom Bulman is Project Director of this innovative initiative, which provides full-time education for disaffected 15-16 year-olds through work experience and core sessions on employability, health and citizenship.

Citischool, based on *City as School* USA and the earlier *Parkway Project* of Philadelphia, is a facility for young people who learn best when working in the wider community. Instead of moving from class to class within one building, students move from workplace to workplace. Learning takes place at a range of locations across the city and involves a range of adults, all experts on the world of work, life and learning. It recognises that what matters most in learning is motivation, how learners feel about themselves and those around them. The students learn individually and co-operatively with the guidance of a personal advisor.

"Citischool is not like an ordinary school. It is about hands on learning and that's good."   (Student, March 2002)

Citischool is a striking · example of a virtual school. It has no buildings of its own. It points the way to a more learner-friendly, personalised, flexible and relevant curriculum.

(*Citischool* has been developed by Countec, Milton Keynes Education Business Partnership and the development is funded by the Learning Skills Council for Milton Keynes, Oxfordshire and Buckinghamshite.   Further information can be found on the website: www.countec.org/citischool.)

Citischool is based on the New York *City as School* project which Tom Bulman visited in November 2000, and describes below:

Gabrielle Hernandez, 17, waits with her father to see her Teacher Advisor. It is parents evening at the cramped headquarters of City-As-School, the work experience school in downtown Manhattan, New York.   Gabrielle rocks her one-year-old child and smiles. *"I've been to five high schools,"* she says, *"and this is the first I've stuck with."*

In an era of school reform dominated by prescribed curricula and standardised testing, City-As-School (CAS) stands out as a public high school with a difference. Instead of attending classes in one building, students attend a series of extended work experience placements averaging 20-32 hours per week. Students gain academic credit for project work on placement. A student may have a programme made up of several short work placements ('learning experiences') or one or two lengthy ones, sometimes beyond the normal school day. Students earn credit only, no pay.

Starting with 15 students and a Ford Foundation grant in 1972, CAS now offers full-time education for over 1,000 students in their final two years of high school, aged 16 and up. Students are referred by mainstream schools where they have not engaged with traditional classroom teaching. *"Some students have learning or behaviour difficulties when they come to us,"* says Bill Weinstein, Resource Services Co-ordinator, *"but many are very bright, some gifted."*

"I consider myself a bright student," says Gabrielle, *"but I'm easily bored. I was kicked out of my last school for fighting with another kid. Here they gave me choices, like a college, and that's what I needed."*

Gabrielle arrived with 20 credits from other schools (students need 40 to graduate US high school). She sat down with her Teacher Advisor to work out an individual learning programme which would cover the credits she needed in English, Social Studies, Maths and Science. Looking through the CAS catalogue of learning resources - over 600 work experience placements in New York City - they found one with a fashion photographer. She collected the Learning Experience Activity Package (LEAP) for that job, outlining the academic task: a daily log, some book research, interviews, photos, an article and a presentation. Most CAS placements last eight weeks, but this was for a double-cycle of 16 weeks, worth four credits in English and Social Studies. Gabrielle attended in-house CAS lessons in Maths and Science, and her Resource Co-ordinator was able to re-negotiate Gabrielle's LEAP with the work experience supervisor to include some science assignments.

Gabrielle's friend, Kathleen Cruz, 19, is soon to graduate from CAS having completed her credit requirement through LEAPs at three learning resource sites, a child care centre, a theatre and a police station. *"There is no limit to the possibilities,"* says Weinstein. *"We always try to fix up Learning Resources that meet the kids' needs. We don't let them do just menial jobs."*

Cruz now plans to be a Maths teacher in Junior High School, something she *"wouldn't have dreamed of"* when she dropped out of her last high school. *"It's a lot to do with the staff here,"* she says. *"Because we call them by their first names, we feel equal to them. They're there to help us, and they really do."* All CAS staff members share responsibility for student guidance. Teacher Advisors have direct contact with a specific group of students, holding weekly meetings to complete journal entries and cover important school business. Resource Co-ordinators look after the placements.

"Making up my own schedule was great," says Cruz. *"And I've become less scared of weird people."*

"There are skaters, hip-hop kids, gangsters, rich white kids, even devil-worshippers...a lot of these kids are trouble-makers, kicked out of their own schools," explains Cruz. *"Like him,"* she laughs, pointing playfully towards her boyfriend, Oswaldo Morales, who is soon to graduate, aged 20, having been kept down a year twice in his 'zone' high school for not completing the required credits. *"But not at City-As,"* Kathleen continues seriously. *"It works here because we choose to do it (the work placements) and they (the staff) treat us with respect."*

Most students come from 'zone' neighbourhood schools beyond wealthy downtown Manhattan. *"There are no fights in this school because we're all out of our neighbourhoods. There are no metal detectors. Zone schools have neighbourhood rivalries. Here you can start over."*

Case study:

Community Arts: definitions and core values
by Mark Webster

How many times have I heard people say *"I can't draw"*? The fact is, that most people do not think they are artistic or that the Arts have much to do with their lives. To many, it is just something that recalls unhappy memories of schooldays. Yet this is interesting, given the fact that we are surrounded by art products. Mass culture has bred a whole generation of art consumers but it has brought little by way of choice or diversity. Neither has it done anything to democratise the Arts or to give people the belief that its production is something in which they can actively participate.

This is not, of course, something peculiar to Britain. All western/northern industrialised countries have demonstrated the same tendency to lodge the power to define and to create art with an educational and economic elite, and to produce a population of art consumers.

Even so, every community has its break dancers, silk painters and poets. People get together to sing, to act and to tell stories - but this creativity tends to go unnoticed and unvalued and finds little representation in official culture. Its importance and significance is largely unrecognised and unacknowledged and, where cultural forms find popularity, they are quickly appropriated or co-opted by the arts establishment or the commercial arts sector.

Community Arts grew in Britain as a movement to try to re-establish the link between people and culture, to stimulate and inspire new types of activity and to value and promote latent or hidden skills and talents in communities. It attempts to give people the tools to be active, confident participators and creators, to help communities discover, develop and use their ability to express themselves through creativity, and to find their voice.

What is Community Arts?

Community Arts is a term embracing all those activities which involve groups of people doing creative things together. What differentiates Community Arts, say, from amateur arts or the professional or commercial arts, is that:

- It promotes participation, regardless of the existing level of skill or 'talent'.

- It is undertaken by a group who either have the same collective identity, or a goal greater than the art form itself, or both.

- It is developed primarily to provide opportunities for people who through economic or social circumstance have little access to the means to participate in the Arts.

The activities are often in the form of projects and (though not exclusively) consist of workshops that lead towards an end event or end product.

The activity itself could be anything from a Community Festival to a book, a video to a dance, a mosaic to a mural, or even a combination of all these and more. Community Arts is not defined by art form but by **process**.

The long term effect of Community Arts work may be the setting up of a self-sustaining activity or permanent group - a writing group in a library perhaps, or a community choir. It may lead a community group to see the potential of the Arts in connection with another activity - a housing campaign, health promotion or the programme of activities for an over-sixties group.

Alternatively, it may provide access to a field of endeavour that an individual felt was previously closed to them - someone who had always enjoyed social dancing goes on to learn Bhanghra or Jazz dance. Also, its long term effect may be simply that individuals feel more empowered and confident to go on to do other things in their lives, like taking part in more community activity or getting involved in local politics or to go into further or higher education.

When projects lead to the setting up of self-sustaining activity or to the opening of a resource, this is usually termed a 'development'. It is work to bring about these 'developments' (i.e. development work) that probably does the most to authenticate Community Arts' claims to make long lasting change, and to differentiate Community Arts from other participative arts activity.

Another feature of Community Arts activity is that at some stage in a project's lifetime it involves the involvement of an artist or an arts worker. This is a breed of people who spend their time and make a living from sharing their skills with people. Their purpose is to enable them to participate in projects, learn skills and share ideas. Often these workers define themselves in terms of art-form specialisms, for example as visual artists, or as 'makers', or performers; or even more specifically, as say, video workers, digital media workers, dancers or textile workers.

Since the scale of much of the work often necessitates the involvement of more than one worker, and a considerable number of resources, teams have grown up which include workers with complimentary arts skills. In addition, projects do not simply spring out of thin air. They need to be administered, co-ordinated and managed.

As a result, the last twenty-five years has seen the rise of another breed of people called Arts Development Workers or Community Arts Development Workers. It is their job to see the potential for projects, to talk to people, to find money, to set up and manage projects and ultimately to identify potential new developments after projects have finished, and to build the outcomes of projects into policies and strategies.

There are several models for the supply of these Community Arts 'services':

Freelance - Where arts workers or development workers work independently, making partnerships with community groups or other arts agencies around specific projects.

Art form agencies - Agencies who specialise in a single art form or activity such as drama, dance or video. Their activities may be linked to a particular facility such as a community dance studio or community video studio, or they may specialise in setting up community-based projects within community facilities. Quite often they do both.

Arts organisations with Community Arts Officers or Education Officers - Within this category are all those organisations whose main activity is not participatory but who want to promote participation in the Arts or increase access to them. Such organisations include theatre groups and art galleries who often describe their work with communities and schools as *Audience Development*.

Community Arts agencies - These are organisations that exist to develop Community Arts activities in a variety of art forms based on community needs. The early model for such organisations when Community Arts as a concept was still finding its feet, was of small companies in the voluntary sector, funded by the then regional arts authorities, and local councils employing workers with a range of art form skills to work within a given catchment area. While such teams still exist, and in some cases have grown quite large, with attendant resource bases and arts centres, the past twenty years has also seen the growth of the local authority sector.

Local authorities

Most of the larger local councils now either have a Community Arts Team, a Community Arts Officer, or an Arts Development Officer who, as part of their brief, have the job of developing Community Arts. While some local authorities actually employ their own art form staff, more usually local authority officers act as brokers between local community needs and the arts organisations, or arts workers within their area. There is no set model for delivery. Sometimes local authorities are direct providers of projects and programmes of activity, while others seek a more developmental approach encouraging partnership, working cross service area within the council or in partnership with other organisations. With the large number of funding sources now available through regeneration frameworks, and of course through the National Lottery, most local authorities have both an advisory and advocacy role in supporting voluntary and community groups in applying for funds to support Community Arts work at a local level. Some local authorities even administer their own grants fund from which it is possible to apply to set up Community Arts activity to local arts organisations.

Increasingly, the pressure is on local authorities to think regionally and to work at a strategic level. Many have argued that this will have the effect of reducing their role as direct service deliverers in the long term. This diversity of practice has led to a wide variance in philosophy, method and approach between local authorities, to the point where it is possible to say that there is no universally understood definition of what the term Community Arts actually means.

Walsall Community Arts Team

Walsall Community Arts Team is a local authority team that, while not unique, represents an important development in the way Community Arts is developed within a geographical area. It was set up in 1989, as part of a new Arts And Cultural Services Division within the brand new Leisure Services Department of Walsall Metropolitan Borough Council. Within the division, alongside the Community Arts Team, was brought the Walsall Art Gallery, the Museums section and, the then, yet to be completed, Walsall Garage, Arts and Media Centre.

Walsall is a large urban conurbation to the north west of Birmingham, consisting of four distinct towns and something around 265,000 people. To the north of the Borough is a large expanse of 1950s council housing where the population is largely white and working class. To the south and west is an area of mixed housing ranging from high rise blocks, to back-to-back terraces, home to a rich mixture of communities and cultures. All the indicators show Walsall to be a place that is economically and socially disadvantaged. By common agreement, it was also a place that in 1989 was starved of resources for the Arts.

The whole arts and cultural development, which emerged out of a process that included a cultural audit and years of planning and negotiating, had a strong community bias, and in this reflected the history and commitment of Walsall Council to producing accessible, relevant, community focused services. The Community Arts Team, therefore, had the advantage of existing within a framework which, in theory at least, valued community-focused work, and put Community Arts work alongside its mainstream services. It was also building on a history of Community Arts provision in the Borough which had been sporadic and piecemeal but which had made some real achievements and demonstrated the potential for development.

In its first incarnation, the Team had four full-time development workers, of which I was one, and a budget to employ freelance arts workers. It was then also part of an agreement with West Midlands Arts and the Regional Arts Board, which would bring extra money into the Borough over the next three years to finance Community Arts developments.

The approach we took from the start was that of active initiators. We did not just want to wait until groups came to us, we believed that the only way we would have an effect was if we went out and found projects to get going. It was also important to us that the service was actually based on people's needs and that we were not simply parachuting in 'arty' projects which we thought would be good for people.

Early attempts to set up projects which reflected people's needs included a Banner Festival on one council estate, which was designed to bring groups together to celebrate their hopes for the future. In another area, we brought in video workers to work with several groups as part of a project to document housing problems, while another community organisation worked on a photographic project which tied into the opening of their community centre and documented their aspirations for the centre.

As our experience grew so did that of the groups we worked with, and soon people came to us to start developing their ideas. While we continued to develop new projects with new groups, there was now also need to set up a support structure which could help groups to develop and manage their own projects.

In the fifteen years of its existence, the Community Arts Team in Walsall has developed a strong philosophy for the provision of this support, or 'development service', and a structure for its delivery. Today, the Team offers a complex programme of development work, advocacy, advice and project delivery across a whole range of agendas.

The key to its strength as it has grown, is that although it now works at a strategic level within the council and across the region it has not lost its personable hands-on approach. A member of the Team could equally find themselves being called to London to advise a government committee one day, be asked to sit in for the council's chief executive on a regional regeneration panel the following day, and then find themselves humping equipment for a community event on the next. That its annual turnover as a team is now well in excess of one million pounds has not meant it has lost any of its grass roots support, and this has been built on the very simple philosophy of agreeing what they are going to do with communities and then delivering it, exactly when and how they said they were going to deliver it.

Over the years the Team has developed some fundamental principles for the practice of Community Arts in Walsall. These are now woven into all of the work of the Team and provide the basis for the arts policy officially adopted by the Council:

- **Empowerment:** that work should empower communities in Walsall
- **Participation:** that work should seek and promote the active participation of communities
- **Access:** that all work promotes greater access to the Arts
- **Quality:** that people in Walsall deserve high quality service
- **Partnership:** that all work is done in partnership with local communities

These principles form the cornerstones on which all the work is now based, and the basis for the development of the Community Arts Service in Walsall. By focusing on these principles in turn, and by exploring the issues that arise out of them, the following chapters of the book aim to explain the power of the Community Arts process to foster change, and its ability to move things on.

(from: Webster, M. and Buglass, G. (2005) *Finding Voices, Making Choices*, Nottingham: Educational Heretics Press)

Chapter six:

The next learning system

John Holt in *Instead of Education* wrote to one young teacher who was asking how he could change the schools:

"You are going to have your hands full, just trying to find or make for yourself a spot in which you can do not too much harm, be reasonably honest with your students, help some of them cope a little better with the problems of school, and get some fun out of your work. To do even that little will not be easy." (p. 209)

Teachers who see themselves as radical rarely changed anything, Holt concluded, and they become frustrated by their failures to teach children to think. They are fooling themselves because they are coerced themselves into doing the business of the school.

It is not likely that a winner-loser society will be radically changed by the winners, and as long as school remains compulsory, coercive and competitive, any changes teachers make will be short-lived, or not go very deep, or not spread very far.

Holt suggests that when more of us ask questions about why all adults should be taxed to provide a system of schools from which the children of the rich and affluent gain the most, in others words, where the poor children always seem to lose, then reform may become possible. In the meantime, teachers can encourage children to have an active learning life outside school:

"All the children I have known who were coping best with school, doing well at it, and more or less happy in it, led the largest and most interesting and important parts of their lives outside of school. Children who do not like school and are not doing well there, but cannot escape it, need such an out-of-school life even more. And children who escape school must have some alternative, some interesting and pleasant (to them) way of spending the time that other children spend in school."
(*Instead of Education*, p. 215)

In addition, the hidden curriculum of the school is best exposed by being honest with children about these matters and expressing healthier values in their own life and work. Often the best thing is to do nothing dramatic, but listen to their children sympathetically, because what a child may need most is what school generally denies them - a chance to tell their story to people who will listen and try to understand. This action by learner-friendly teachers shows that they take their feelings seriously, and this alone may be enough to help their children make the best of it. (For further ideas on helping children, parents and teachers survive schooling, see Meighan, R. (2004) *Damage Limitation*, Educational Heretics Press.)

Apart from that, teachers can help by showing their children some of the tricks that will help them play the school game better. The children can be helped to realise that the school game is as unreal and abstract as chess, but beating it requires the learning of the tricks. As one said to me, *"Now I know other people think it is senseless too, I can bear it."* Useless though most of it is, there are rewards of a kind for playing it well, those of college and university entrance and the job tickets.

There are various groups around the world that have been at work on ideas for a new learning system suitable for the next century. They include the Educational Futures Project USA, Education 2000 UK, Education Now UK, TRANET International based in the USA, and AERO USA. For example, the TRANET annual report for 1996 says:

"Thinkers in every walk of life are recognising that our current form of governance threatens ecological, political, social, and economic failure ... Management guru Peter Drucker says in his Post Capitalist Society 'there is a need to restore community.' He sees a new community-centred society ... in which schools are replaced by an open life-long learning system which any person can enter, at any level, any time ...

"The 'Learning Community' theme is echoed by holistic educators who now recognise that 'child-centred education', much as it is needed for the flexibility inherent in the age ahead, is inconsistent with 'schooling'. 'Teaching' or 'schooling' implies that society, or someone is acting on, indoctrinating some amorphous blobs. 'Learning', on the other hand, implies a self-actualised process of creating skills, taking in knowledge, and satisfying one's natural curiosity ... Learning, like politics must be reinvented.

"The vision of a 'World Without Schools' is being developed by organisations such as the Educational Futures Project. Schools fade into the background as the community as a whole becomes a network of learning centres; and the people themselves take

*control of their own and their family's whole-life learning.
Museums, libraries, churches, businesses, YMCAs and a growing
set of other learning centres, (mental fitness centres not unlike
today's physical fitness centres), provide all citizens with the
knowledge they need for their own right livelihood ... 'mentors'
(whom we now call 'teachers') provide a personal consulting and
advisory service to people of all ages.   They keep detailed
databases on learning opportunities throughout the region and
by counselling and guidance help each family and individual
reach self-set goals for gaining knowledge ... "*
                                   William. N. Ellis, editor of *TRANET*

In *Smart Schools, Smart Kids*, (1992) Edward Fiske, New York
Times educational editor, reports that US press correspondents met
to review the results of five years of educational reform. They
began to suspect that things were worse instead of better. Fiske
went on tour to try to find something more positive. He concluded:

*"Trying to get more learning out of the current system is like
trying to get the Pony Express to compete with the telegraph by
breeding faster ponies."*

Fiske advocated a complete rethink of the fundamental assumptions
of our obsolete model of schooling.

Sir Christopher Ball, former Director of Learning for the Royal
Society of Arts writing in the *RSA Journal*, December 1995, p.6,
makes the following observation:

*"I realised that I am among those who believe that Tomorrow's
School will be a replacement for, not merely an adjustment of,
today's system of education."*

John Abbott, Director of Education 2000 in *Education 2000 News*
September 1996, added his voice:

*"Mounting evidence world-wide suggests that traditional
education systems are becoming increasingly dysfunctional in
the face of escalating technological, social, and economic
change. Education systems based on out-of-date or incomplete
assumptions about how people learn can, unwittingly, create and
perpetuate dependent societies.   People who come to see
themselves as 'learning failures' when young have no confidence
in their ability to embrace change as adults."*

Some industrial concerns in the USA are now supporting approaches with grants designed to:

> *"enable those entrepreneurs and risk-takers in education to break up the institutional gridlock that has stifled innovation and creativity."*

These were the comments of Nabisco's chairman, Louis V. Gerstner.

In the Co-operative Society's Members magazine for Spring 1996, Byron Henderson, Director of the Centre for the Study of Co-operatives, Canada writes:

> *"Home schooling ... may well be at the forefront of school change ... The Wall Street Journal's electronic edition recently ran the story of a 13 year-old student in New York State who does not travel to a classroom, but instead uses his computer a third of his study day, to access books, encyclopaedias on CD-ROM ... and the Internet, to meet friends, discuss classes and prepare reports ... Multi-media distance education and the Internet are coming to public awareness and they offer the prospect of both better education and lower cost."*

John Taylor Gatto in his book *Dumbing Us Down: the hidden curriculum of compulsory schooling,* concludes that schooling in the USA is a twelve year jail sentence where, *"bad habits are the only curriculum truly learned",* and that school 'schools' very well, but hardly educates at all. It is time for drastic changes, he concludes.

As noted earlier, bullying is embedded in the model of schooling currently employed in the UK because it operates as a **bully institution** - the compulsory day-prison, employs **a bully curriculum** - the compulsory National Curriculum, enforced by the increasingly favoured **bully pedagogy** of teacher-dominated formal teaching, and reinforced by the **bully compulsory assessment system**. In the UK this is all reinforced by a **bully schools inspection service** until recently led by a man who has declared in public meetings that *'fear is a great motivator'* - one of the classic doctrines of fascist-tending regimes that teaches that adults get their way by bullying - psychological, institutional, physical, or otherwise. (See Harber, C., *Schooling as Violence*, Routledge, 2004)

Alice Miller reminds us that every bully was once a victim, for bullying is learnt behaviour. Until we replace our current morbid model with a new model of a flexible learning system based on democratic principles, the root causes of bullying will continue.

1. Some key ideas for the next learning system

(a) Learner-managed learning

Home-based educating families tend to take it for granted that the learners will manage their own learning, at first in style and soon after that in content. This is often achieved on a trial and error basis.

(b) A network of learning sites

In the proposed Minnesota Experimental City, planned as a laboratory for social, technical, economic and environmental innovations, a new approach to education is proposed. The following *Learning Centres* are to be developed to replace the current model of custodial schools:

- **Early life studios** will be designed so that parents, young children and staff members could meet regularly to create an environment that provided creative learning experiences and offer opportunities for parents and older young people and other adults to learn about the mental, emotional, physical and other needs of early childhood.

- **Stimulus studios** will be established where there would be a constantly changing array of prompts to provoke and extend learners' perceptions and thinking, to arouse curiosity, stimulate laughter, wonder, reverence, imagination and competence. There would be films, tapes, videos, exhibitions, books, resourceful people from the community, and virtual reality experiences.

- **Gaming studios** will be established where learning takes place by playing educational games and there is the opportunity to take part in simulations and role play. Arena theatre events will also be developed and presented.

- **Project studios** will be available where learners work on real projects such as making a video, writing a book or TV script, designing new materials and products, or planning projects to be undertaken later in the community. In the UK, Walsall Community Arts has produced a *Dreaming for Real* project pack which has been setting such projects in motion. (See Webster M., and Buglass, G., *Finding Voices, Making Choices,* 2005 Educational Heretics Press.)

- **Learner banks** will be designed to store and loan out the tools and equipment needed by learners. A large part of the bank would store books and other material now found in conventional libraries.

- **Family-life centres** will be set up where families will learn together. The centre will offer meetings, seminars, tutoring or community-centred discussions. Provision will be made here for those who learn well for some of the time in school-type settings.

- **Community facilities** such as homes, businesses, public places, sports facilities, will be available as appropriate, as part of the learning network. The network of learning centres will remain permanently fluid, open to evaluation, review and change. (See Glines, D. and Long K. (1992) 'Transitioning Towards Educational Futures' *Phi Delta Kappen* March 1992.)

In the new learning system, it is *learning* that is the central concern and not teaching. Every person is simultaneously a learner *and* a resource person for the learning of others.

When I was collecting information from home-educating families in the late 1970s and 1980s, I found that I had to do most of my visits on Sundays. This was · because whenever I telephoned to fix appointments, I would find that the learners were learning out-and-about in various libraries, museums, exhibitions, gatherings such as auctions, expeditions, sports centres, meetings with adults who had offered some learning opportunity, and the like. They had already taken on the idea of the community as a source of learning sites.

(c) The Catalogue Curriculum

When I wrote about the Catalogue Curriculum idea in 1995, Don Glines of the Educational Futures Project, USA, wrote about his experience of using such an approach in his US High School:

> *"We found the 'window shopping and shopper's guide' notions helpful in the first year and for new students, but once the programme was rolling, the students just developed all their own studies and planned their own self-directed curriculum experiences ... even the 'low achievers' really take off when they finally learn that you **are** telling the truth - that they **can** create their own learning based upon interests and success."*

I can accept what Glines is saying here. When I gave student teachers choice about how to organise their initial teacher education course, the same thing happened - fifteen times in fifteen years. But 'the catalogue' enabled them to locate the best option for them.

(d) Personal learning plans

The Royal Society of Arts promoted the idea of personal learning plans as part of an educational initiative. The director of the project, Sir Christopher Ball, saw the aim of the project as creating a learning culture in Britain. By implication, years of compulsory mass schooling have done no such thing.

(e) Direct access to the information-rich society

Seymour Papert in *Mindstorms* forecast how computer technology would change things by modifying the environment outside classrooms:

"I believe that the computer presence will enable us to so modify the learning environment outside the classroom that much, if not all, the knowledge schools presently try to teach with such pain and expense and such limited success will be learned, as the child learns to walk, painlessly, successfully, and without organised instruction.

"This obviously implies that schools, as we know them today, will have no place in the future. But it is an open question whether they will adapt by transforming themselves into something new or wither away and be replaced."

(f) Teachers as learning agents

In John Adcock's book *In Place of Schools* he develops the idea of a new role for teachers. The model would be that of family doctors operating in health centres. The new teacher would not work in a school but in a centre, or from their homes, or both, and their concern would be to help devise and service the personal learning plans of a group of clients.

For my own part, I prefer a slightly different model - that of the travel agent. Teachers as learning agents would operate from their 'learning travel bureau' helping any learner to 'visit' and explore any learning that was chosen.

(g) Assessment on request

Philip Gammage observed that: *"Nobody grew taller by being measured."* This would seem to put assessment firmly in its place as a mass schooling fetish.

There are, however, several provisos. Systems such as the education systems of the Scandinavian countries certainly manage perfectly well without anything like external examinations such as the UK's GCSE and GCE 'A' levels. But they introduce vocational tests post-schooling on the sensible grounds that people who provide services in society need to be appropriately qualified e.g. nobody I know wants their teeth attended to by unqualified people.

In addition, testing can be available on request. The grades for musical instrument proficiency are example of such tests. The 'on request' is, however, crucial. As a jazz musician myself, of somewhat modest achievement, who does not read music, the tests are no use to me, nor do I desire them. A compulsory testing system would, erroneously, identify me as a non-musician.

2. The old and new systems compared

With some key concepts now established, we can juxtapose the assumptions of the current compulsory mass schooling system with those of the next learning system. The mass schooling system assumes that:

- Learning is preparation for life, so at some point learning stops and living starts.
- Learning occurs mostly in school.
- Specialists are needed to impart knowledge.
- Education takes place in a school and requires a prescribed curriculum.
- People do not and cannot learn on their own.
- People with a large quantity of memorised information are better people than those with less.
- Schools are needed to socialise and civilise.

The next learning system, on the other hand, assumes that:

- Learning is life, because humans are learning animals and, whilst we are alive, we are learning.
- Learning occurs everywhere and anywhere.
- People can direct their own learning.
- Education is a lifelong activity that needs to be personalised using a Catalogue Curriculum.
- People can learn to make decisions on what and how to learn.
- Everyone is important regardless of how much they have memorised.
- People are socialised and get civilised in their communities.

The trailblazing activity of the home-based educating families now begins to become clear because they have already been 'field testing' most of the components of the new system for almost twenty years, without necessarily having this as a conscious intention.

3. Home-based educating families in co-operation

Some home-based educating families are already busily developing learning clubs, family centres and other forms of co-operative learning as the following accounts demonstrate:

(a) The Otherwise Club
(see also Case Study in Chapter 4)

"In February 1993 we set up *The Otherwise Club* as a centre for families of children educated out of school and committed to some vision of alternative education. It evolved out of a small learning club at one parent's house in which children from home-based educating families were able to work together regularly on interesting projects. The group was set up with two basic aims:

- to provide for regular social interaction where families can exchange views and ideas. This is something we feel causes concern to those considering home education;

- to provide workshops and group activities in which members can participate. This aspect of educating out of school for many families requires most effort and organisation.

Our premises are in Kilburn where we hire a hall and several rooms and a kitchen for two days a week. There are also specialist areas for woodwork, photographic developing and pottery available. We have about 20 families who pay £100 per year to cover basic costs. Workshops have been enjoyed on first aid, philosophy for children and stained glass work. Forthcoming workshops include computers and rock climbing. Drama, pottery and the production of a newsletter are regular activities. Parents talking to parents and exchanging experiences about home-based education is a regular but non-scheduled vital activity. The whole family can learn together and also socialise with other families.

The *Otherwise Club* is run collectively, with all members having equal access to setting the agenda and to the decision-making process. There is a fortnightly meeting and a key planning meeting every half term."

(Above extract is from the leaflet describing The *Otherwise Club* which can be obtained by sending a stamped addressed envelope to: Leslie Barson, 1 Croxley Road, London W1 3HH)

(b) The Isle of Wight Learning Zone
by Rob Alexander

The *Isle of Wight Learning Zone* (IWLZ) is a group of over 40 home educating families offering support, resources and social contacts. Of course, that is the very basic essence of what we are actually all about. The group was conceived on a July evening in 1999 when a few home educators got together to discuss, as they had for some time, issues like dealing with the LEA and the possible need for a small school. We left that meeting with the germ of an idea that in September 1999 became IWLZ, with the grand total of six families. We had identified that, while we were all coping well enough on our own, children and adults alike might benefit from activities that brought in new people, new ideas. We also felt that there were other families out there, unhappy with school or who wanted to home educate but who needed someone to talk to, someone to give them support, encouragement and inspiration.

Three practical ideas helped tie us together as a group. The first was that when we did something creative, broadly educational or just plain fun with our children, we could offer a few places to other children in the IWLZ. The second was a newsletter that would help publicise these activities and keep members in touch. The third was regular committee meetings at a child-friendly venue, which helped us thrash out the beginnings of a constitution. These meetings were where we met new members and really got to know old ones, and where many friendships have been formed. Within two months, we had embarked on the first of many wildly ambitious projects, a play written and performed by the children, which was performed in public. Weeks started to fill up with workshops and socials, children enlarged their social contacts and began to participate in many new activities, and the committee expanded. The number of families increased rapidly, until it stabilised at about 30. Big projects like the first play have both pulled us together and challenged us all. Over the last year, we have organised camping and walking trips, socials, many workshops, a cardboard boat regatta, an adventure weekend, a science access course, an art exhibition and a choir, to name just a few activities. A core of hardworking committee members work on producing the newsletter every two months and a bulletin of events in between. An events co-ordinator keeps track of workshops and events, people deal with publicity, committee meetings, the LEA, letters, grants, new members, money etc. in their own time, as well as keeping the energy flowing round the group. But it is the members who set up a workshop or event (or who attend them) who actually keep the IWLZ going. From the very start, we have built in the principle of acceptance, inclusion, non-judgement. It is OK to send a child to school, it is OK to have special needs in the group, it is OK to fail within the *Learning Zone*. In this environment, many children have flourished, trying new things, gaining friends, learning new skills.

But I think the adults have gained as much. At *Zone* workshops or socials, home education is the norm, we are not the odd ones out. Other parents offer support without judgement when we falter or question. We have had opportunities to share our interests and our ideas without ridicule. That is not to say we do not have lively debates, even heated ones, but these happen when people care deeply about things. They are a bit like family disputes, they have to be thrashed out in order to move on again. *The Zone* has proved itself, after several years, to be a robust, optimistic group full of energy, positivity and love. I look forward to the next few years.

(c) The South Downs Learning Centre
by Ian Cunningham

Children taking charge of their own learning? Can it be possible? **YES.** We've been developing the **Self Managed Learning** approach over many years – and it works. The *South Downs Learning Centre* is a new venture, initiated by the *Centre for Self Managed Learning* in Brighton, which is based on these principles. **Self Managed Learning** does what it says on the label – it helps people to be more self managing. Young people become more self confident, more able to take charge of their own lives and more likely to pursue satisfying careers.

Many people have taken their children out of school because they do not feel that their children are getting the chance to learn the things they want in the way they want. Other children stay in school but want a chance to take more control of their own lives. We can support both groups of parents and children. The Learning Centre provides programmes during the week for children being home educated and also weekend groups for those in school.

The Centre opened in 2003 year with a group of 12 to 15 year-olds (the initial target age-range is 7 to 16 year-olds). There is no imposed curriculum and students agree their own learning goals with the group and with their parents. The group meet one day a week in a Community Learning Centre and for the rest of the week students work in whatever location suits them – often at home – but students also go to tutors, do attachments such as to the RSPCA, play music and visit each other. Most students intend to do some GCSEs but they are learning a whole lot more than the ability to pass examinations.

The *South Downs Learning Centre* is developing an active community where people feel part of something worthwhile.

(For more info contact Ian on 01273 703691 or
cunningham@pavilion.co.uk)

(d) The Stables Project, York
by Linda Fryer

The Stables Project, is a small centre working essentially, but not exclusively, with young people. We are housed in an old stables block converted into two studio spaces with small darkroom, kitchen, workshop, computer room and yard. We are city based, experiential, and determined to respond creatively to modern conditions.

Our first intention was to work with 16-25 year-olds with a focus on orientation in life but were soon joined full-time by 4 fifteen-year-olds, and regular part-timers up to 60 years old. With this first group of 10-14 people we established our particular culture: we all wanted to study, both individually and within interest groups and support each other in documenting our work. The creation of portfolios has since become almost a religion! Through studying human physiology, psychology, history of art and earth sciences, we began to find our own approach to learning within wide age-range groups. We were clear we wanted to explore a host of crafts. We built a wooden lathe that has been used in various furniture and design projects. Afternoon courses have included car mechanics, basketry, lamp making, puppetry designing and making blinds for the studio windows. Friday morning sees us all cleaning the building, reviewing and previewing each week's work, conducting group meetings and regular mentoring sessions.

In summer we presented our puppet theatre as work in progress to local school children, then worked with two artists on projects inspired by the people and places in our immediate locality. We finally opened our doors to our neighbouring public as a gallery, exhibiting final pieces, called *Insite*. During the holidays a group of 20+ year-olds went to work with gypsy children in Romania.

Our discovery of *The Centre for Personalised Education Trust* provided us with timely support, both practically and morally. We have begun to collaborate with other local initiatives and care professionals, have won a substantial grant for this year's community arts project, and have attracted more students. We are now busy consolidating and expanding. We welcome contact!

(Tel: 01904 675 522 or email: stables.project@btclik.com)

(e) Flexi-time schooling

Flexi-time is part-time attendance at school using schools just as they are. It can be seen as a temporary expedient for those who cannot wait for a new system to get established, but for various reasons, do not want to home-educate full-time.

School becomes one of many resources, such as libraries, radio, television, computers, etc., to be used when the child and parent choose, according to a contract between them and the school. The parents are as equally involved as the teachers in the education of the child, whilst the children are encouraged to learn for themselves as well as being taught.

Any school can accommodate flexi-time if it wishes to, but under current law, no school is obliged to do so. The Education Act 1993 (Part IV, subsection 298, No.1) applies:

> *"A local education authority may make arrangements for the provision of suitable full-time or part-time education otherwise than at school for those young persons who, by reason of illness, exclusion from school or otherwise, may not for any period receive suitable education unless such arrangements are made for them."*

Kate Oliver writes of her experience:

> *"At the school where my children attend on an agreed flexi-time basis, they are recorded as 'educated off-site' which is classified as an 'authorised absence'. This means that the funding is exactly as for a full-time student and the school returns are not affected. In the USA, however, the funding is split between the school and the home in the 'Independent Study Programs', as*

such arrangements are called. In California, specially trained staff work out appropriate flexible study plans with the parents and children who want this arrangement. Thus a personal learning plan or learning contract formalises the practical arrangements as regards attendance and learning activity. I also agreed to serve as a school governor."

(Kate Oliver is willing to share her experiences of negotiating and implementing flexi-time schooling. Write to her at 21 St. Mary's Crescent, Leamington Spa, CV31 1JL)

(e) Uppattinas Educational Resource Centre

The re-creation of the Uppattinas school came after a long and painful struggle when the members faced up to the fact that there just were not enough students who could pay sufficient tuition fees, or families who could work hard enough to make up for the shortfall in finances, to sustain the needs of the physical plant, or the teachers required for maintaining it as a 'school'. But it was possible to sustain the physical plant and preserve the integrity of its original commitment to open education through establishing it as a Learning Resource Centre which could be a 'school' or 'un-school', depending on the needs of the members. The director of the centre, Sandy Hurst, explains:

"That was a direction in which I was headed personally and something into which I could put the energy needed for organisation and direction. This could once again be a place to which people came who truly wanted to learn and to share what they had learned."

Based on the idea that we learn everywhere so school is everywhere, then the new Uppattinas is a part of that learning and is still a school. It continues to be a centre for people who want to make contact with others, for learning and sharing, for doing group projects or individual projects, for meeting and for growing together. It is not circumscribed by age limits or time limits. Everyone is welcome and the facility is open to community members as and when they need it. Programmes are limited only by the interests and needs of those involved.

The centre of activities has become families who educate their children at home and use the centre to augment their programmes of study, and students who come to the centre for classes. Workshops and special activities like music and drama are arranged as they are needed by the community. Facilities are available for group meetings large and small, and for many kinds of activities for people of all ages. Workshops have been organised ranging from music improvisation to American Indian survival skills; projects on a variety of environmental concerns; and classes spanning American Literature to First Aid. A list of teachers available to those who need them is kept up-to-date.

The work of the centre is growing and developing and its members currently see it as,

> *"a doing centre for all ages, a repository for tools for doing things, a repository for records of things done, a place for sharing, a source of helpers, a centre for people from all cultures, a source for participant controlled learning, a centre for all who believe in life-long learning."*

(Uppattinas Educational Resource Centre, Glenmoore, PA, USA as described in *The Freethinkers' Pocket Directory to the Educational Universe*, Educational Heretics Press 1995)

Summary

Some of the components of the next learning system are now becoming clearer, and they include:

- Learner-managed learning.
- A network of learning sites.
- The Catalogue Curriculum.
- Personal learning plans.
- Direct access to the information-rich society.
- Teachers as learning agents.
- Parents as 'residential' learning agents.
- Assessment on request.

The change in approach has begun to be noted:

> *"In the 20th century, provision has come before clients. You designed the courses and then tried to find some students to fill them. It is the other way round in the future: find the clients, find out what they want and need and then design (or redesign) your provision."*
>
> (Sir Christopher Ball, in RSA Journal, Nov. 1966, p.9)

As the evidence in this book suggests, the home-based educators are well ahead in developing and field-testing many of the features listed above. Indeed, they are blazing a trail to the next learning system and it is high time we learnt some important lessons from their success.

Chapter seven:

'What is and what might be': personalised education as learner-managed learning instead of government-directed learning

What Is and What Might Be was the title of a book by chief inspector of schools, Edmond Holmes, published in 1911. Holmes had spent 30 years trying to make the first National Curriculum work, along with its testing, its payment by results and its aggressive inspection regime. He finally came to the conclusion that he was ashamed to have been a party to it in a later book entitled *The Tragedy of Education*.

I thought I would borrow the title from Edmond Holmes to show the difference between personalised education as learner-directed learning, and the current orthodoxy of government-directed learning.

The current profile of an individual's learning journey in the UK, for the first stages of his/her life looks like this:

One to four/five years:	Home-based learning with play-group experience, and/or child-minding and nursery experience in some cases.
At four/five years:	Attendance at a state school with a government-dictated curriculum, testing, and inspection with a teacher-directed learning regime, apart from small minorities who attend private schools, or are home-educated by family choice.
At six years:	the same
At seven years:	the same
At eight years:	the same
At nine years:	the same
At ten years:	the same

At eleven years:	the same
At twelve years:	the same
At thirteen years:	the same
At fourteen years:	the same
At fifteen years:	the same
At sixteen years:	Some continue with the same, some leave school and go into employment.
At seventeen years:	the same
At eighteen years:	Approaching half the population go to a university where they study a lecturer-directed learning regime with university-dictated course contents and testing. A growing minority are choosing the more learner-friendly regime of the Open University at a fraction of the debt incurred from the old-style, 'late-adolescent three-year exile' university course.

Within this time period, some will have had some true educational experiences: *"Some true educational experiences are bound to occur in schools. They occur, however, despite and not because of school."* (Everett Reimer)   But, overall, none of this has much to do with personalised learning. It is people processing. It has been said that education is properly defined as *'asking questions all the time'*. The profile above is based on the idea of NOT asking questions but learning the required material, and developing only the required skills, hence the description of it by Paul Goodman as *'compulsory mis-education'*.

From the point of view of personalised education, what are the possible building blocks of a learner-managed education? I will call these 'episodes' and they are organised in one year building blocks. But such episodes could be shorter – a half year or a quarter of a year. These building blocks can be seen as the macro-level of the Catalogue Curriculum, the alternative to an imposed, dictated curriculum. The micro-level contains the more detailed items of the content of experiences, projects, courses and, where appropriate, subjects – the whole range of all possible learning experiences available in society, including the methods of invited teaching, research, books, computers, workshops, and so on.

Here is a list of possible 'episodes':

1.   Home-based education – properly acknowledged and supported

2. Home-based education learning co-operatives
3. Weekday programmes at Community Learning Centres (schools recycled into non-ageist centres)
4. Weekend programmes at local Community Learning Centres
5. Travel and Study year UK
6. Travel and Study year Europe
7. Travel and Study year elsewhere
8. Residential College year with a sports focus (recycled residential school like the Danish EFTA Skole)
9. Residential College year with an arts focus
10. Residential College year with a music and dance focus
11. Residential College year with a rural studies and environmental focus
12. Year for exploration of the learner's locality and its learning sites
13. Joining a Democratic Learning Co-operative based on the local Community Learning Centre or public library
14. Joining a *City as School* scheme
15. Duke of Edinburgh's Award Scheme year or a Scouts, Guides or Woodcraft Folk year
16. Voluntary work in the community
17. Joining an ICT Virtual Learning community or programme such as *NotSchoolNet*.

I am sure readers could add further options to this list.

One learning profile, as decided by the learner in conjunction with the family and a support and advice service of a new profession of personal tutor-guides, might look like this. These would be pedagogues or PEDAs for short, who would act more frequently as educational travel agents than as instructors:

Years one to five:	Home-based learning with play-group experience, and/or child-minding and nursery experience in some cases
Year six:	Further home-based education and involvement in a home-based education learning co-operative
Year seven:	Weekend programmes at local Community Learning Centres with further home-based learning
Year eight:	Weekday programmes at local Community Learning Centres
Year nine:	Year for exploration of the learner's locality and its learning sites

Year ten:	Residential College year with a rural studies and environmental focus
Year eleven:	Weekday programmes at local Community Learning Centres
Year twelve:	Weekday programmes at local Community Learning Centres
Year thirteen:	Residential College year with a music and dance focus
Year fourteen:	Joining a Democratic Learning Co-operative based on the local Community Learning Centres or public library
Year fifteen:	Joining an ICT virtual learning community scheme e.g. *NotSchoolNet*
Year sixteen:	*City as School* scheme combined with voluntary work in the community and involvement in a Community Arts project
Year seventeen:	Residential College year with a sports focus with some music and dance
Year eighteen:	Travel and Study year UK
Year nineteen:	Open University studies along with a Travel and Study year Europe.

At the outset of such an 'episodes' scheme, many families may ask for the familiar pattern of weekday provision for many of the years. This would be available, on request, in a flexible learning system, with the pattern decided by the learners and their families in conjunction with their personal tutor. But, if the experience of the all-year-round education schemes in the USA is anything to go by, the delight of the first families to vary their pattern is catching.

Such a scheme would also need new structures for its implementation. In a letter to the *Times Educational Supplement* in June 2002, I made the following suggestions:

"My own practical three point plan is :

Close down the Department of Education and Skills and all its domination-riddled apparatus including OFSTED, Curriculum and Standards and its totalitarian model of teacher training. They have taken us back to the school system of the 1900s which the Chief Inspector of the time, Edmond Holmes, finally condemned as the 'Tragedy of Education' for its stultifying National Curriculum and learner-hostile approach.

Hand over all school buildings and staff to the Public Library Service with the brief to augment their existing invitational reading and information services to develop a comprehensive service of classes, courses and learning experiences in local community centres for personalised learning, responding to the requests and needs of the learners of all ages. The approach of the Public Library Service, after all, is already the customised one, which is why it is our most popular learning institution. They will need at least two kinds of teacher, some 'sages on the stage' offering taught courses, and rather more personal tutor/teachers to be 'guides on the side', supporting personal learning plans i.e. John Adcock's learning coaches (as in his book Teaching Tomorrow*).*

Open a new Department for the Encouragement of Learning to signal a radical change in philosophy from mass coercive schooling, to open, all-age, local community centres for personalised education, designed to support life-long learning for the multiple educational purposes of employment, citizenship, parenting and personal development.

"These developments will need to be monitored and researched and I recommend that suitable people be recruited from the home-based education movement and also the Open University, or so now since these two groups have been operating the most modern and successful forms of learning for twenty-five years. "

The two systems outlined above produce different kinds of people. The repetitive pattern of the current model brings to mind the comment of John Holt that schooling is really a long drawn-out course in practical slavery:

"What it all boils down to is, are we trying to raise sheep - timid, docile, easily driven or led - or free men? If what we want are sheep, our schools are perfect as they are. If what we want is free men, we'd better start making some big changes. "
(The Underachieving School, p. 36)

The second system, the learner-managed system, is more likely to produce confident, capable researchers with the ability to co-operate with others and institutions as and when necessary. It does not look like the conventional view of a 'balanced curriculum'. But then, I have long held the view that the 'balanced curriculum' was just a superstition or an adult hang-up with no basis in realty. For example, Patrick Moore, the astronomer, was educated at home and did not go to university. He tells us that he chose his curriculum at the age of seven as learning to type, which he thought would be useful, by copy typing some tomes in astronomy. This, he thought, would inform him about the subject that interested him, and would also serve as a course in improving his English. He would also spend some time on his xylophone and later the piano developing his musical skills. This unbalanced curriculum served him well, he explains, since the central activities if his life have been astronomy, journalism and music.

In the second system, the learners manage their learning programmes by exercising choice, with support and guidance. Indeed, an alternative title for this article might have been 'real choice in education'.

Personalised learning, using a system based on the learning episodes approach, could move us into a new, exciting and vibrant education landscape.

Chapter eight:

Conclusion:
why not move to a learning
system fit for a democracy?

The title of this book might be somewhat misleading. 'Good, bad, ugly' are somewhat emotive terms, and 'counter-productive' disguises the key issue as to whether the particular learning system you are looking at is 'fit for purpose'. John Holt declared that schools were not a good idea gone wrong, but a bad idea from the outset. But this statement needs a caveat, which is, 'in a democracy'.

In a democracy, schools are a bad idea from the outset, but in a totalitarian society they are an excellent idea where the purpose is to produce a particular kind of people. They are those who are conformist, fatalistic to the will of the elite, gullible to the dictates of the rulers, ageist in attitude, and who, generally 'know their place' in a clearly stratified society.

This raises a few awkward questions such as, *'why is a totalitarian-sympathetic learning system operating in what likes to call itself a democracy?'* Does this mean that this is really a rudimentary form of democracy and may even be merely pre-democratic, constantly regressing to non-democratic formulations? Or, that the leaders do not want more than a very primitive form of democracy? (Or, as Tony Benn suggests, they loathe democracy and its ideas of power-sharing.)

There are a few clues that this might be the case, for such a society might, irrationally, maintain a monarchy, or have a non-elected second chamber of government, or run a special set of schools specifically to reproduce members of an elite with strong authoritarian tendencies. Its state schools may suddenly decide to make uniforms compulsory, and institute drug tests for the inmates.

In my earlier book, *The Next Learning System*, the ten or so time switches of change that will move learning systems into more fluid patterns are given. **Five** have been noted as of major significance:

a. We now have an information-rich society with direct access through information communications technology.
When mass schooling was established, people lived in an information-poor environment. Since then, radio, television, the explosion of specialist magazines, computers, videos and the like, have all provided the means of making most of the products of the knowledge explosion readily available to anyone who wants them. This is just one of the reasons why home-based education is so successful.

b. We now know much more about how the brain actually works.
The new technologies allow us to watch a living brain at work. As a result, most of the assumptions of behavioural and cognitive psychology are in question. The brain, amongst other things, is better at **pattern-making** than **pattern-receiving.**

c. We now know of thirty different learning styles in humans.
It follows that any uniform approach is intellectual death to some, and often most, of the learners, and is therefore suspect.

d. We now know of at least seven types of intelligence.
Howard Gardner in his book *The Unschooled Mind* (1994), reports his work on multiple intelligences. Seven types of intelligence (analytical, pattern, musical, physical, practical, intra-personal, and inter-personal) are identifiable. Only the first is given serious attention in most schools. Yet, we now know that so-called 'ordinary' people are capable of feats of intellectual or creative activity in rich, challenging, non-threatening, co-operative learning environments, and that the narrow competitive tests currently in use to achieve 'the raising of standards' just prevent this from happening.

e. Home-based education has proved to be remarkably successful.
There are a clutch of reasons why this is so, but a significant one is the use of **purposive conversation** as a learning method, in substitution for most formal teaching. Self-managed learning is another to replace teacher-directed instruction. A learner-

friendly setting, efficient use of time, toleration of different learning styles, multiple intelligences, are amongst others.

In 2004, Professor Ted Wragg proposed that we do away with OFSTED, SATS and league tables. A bolder, more radical approach is to phase out mass coercive schooling altogether. It is, after all, a learning system from last century devised in the previous century to cope with an information-poor society and the needs of industrialisation. Even during the last century it was described as 'compulsory mis-education' (Paul Goodman), 'the tragedy of education' (Edmond Holmes) and 'the betrayal of youth' (James Hemming). It was devised for totalitarian not democratic societies, which is why it was so popular with leaders such as Stalin and Hitler.

I believe that the current situation now shames us all. I never thought, as a young teacher setting out on my career over forty years ago, that I would live to see:

- a parent sent to prison because her children were too unhappy at school to attend,
- a teacher sent to prison for cheating in examinations,
- head teachers dismissed for cheating,
- a school that refused the SATS 'fined' £3000 of their annual allocation until they caved in,
- cases of teachers taking their own lives because of the oppressiveness of the inspection service OFSTED,
- a teacher setting fire to a school, joining the ranks of pupils who do so,
- police patrols to round up school refusers,
- a proposal that head teachers issue £50 fines to parents in respect of truancy,
- head teachers to fine parents up to £100 for taking their children away on holiday in term time without permission,
- about a third of all teachers wishing to leave teaching as soon as possible,
- 31% of young parents with pre-school age children having so little regard for schools that they are considering home-based education. And, 61% of these not long after experiencing the system for themselves, saying they have little trust in the education system to provide a decent education (Vauxhall Centenary Parents Survey, 2002),

• random drugs testing proposed for children in school.

Any one of these facts taken individually might not signify much, but taken together they indicate that something is fundamentally wrong with the current learning system which is based on 'children in captivity' type schooling, using coercion and heavy with domination. In contrast to these totalitarian charateristics, Nelson Mandela's choice for his Minister of Education, Professor Bengu, declared that 'democracy means the **absence of domination**'.

Professor Ted Wragg, writing in the Times Educational Supplement (7/9/04) asked the question,

> *"How on earth have we reached a situation where every tiny detail in education is laid down by the state?"*

He goes on to say,

> *"In 1980, I wrote an article entitled 'State-approved knowledge: 10 steps down the slippery slope'. It was intended as a dire warning that a determined government could seize control of education and the minds of those within it ... By the early 1990s, all ten steps of my Orwellian nightmare were in place as the Conservative government introduced a legally enforced state curriculum, state tests, league tables, etc. Step 10 was reached when the first teachers were sacked for not teaching the national curriculum. Ministers took 366 additional powers in the 1988 Education Act, and their successors followed suit. Today state control is regarded as the norm.*

> *"Recently I was asked to devise 10 further steps, but I refused. The original, meant to be a horror story, had become a blueprint ... Anyway, the next ten steps are already there. Step 12 or so would be the state-decreed minute by minute lesson plans – i.e. the literacy hour. Step 14 might be the 117-item state assessment schedule for five-year-olds. Step 16-ish is the hundreds of competencies prescribed for trainee teachers. Step 18 is the 2002 Education Act requirement to send in a form to the minister if you want to innovate. Step 20 came when state bureaucracy finally became satire as the government set*

*up two committees to look into the problem of
duplication."*

Could we move away from the totalitarian-style learning system
now in place to something that looked like education? Ted
Wragg is pessimistic:

*"There is one huge obstacle. Power is a narcotic. For
years politicians have become addicted to it in education.
No sooner had the government announced schools were
going to be set free, than ministers were telling heads they
must introduce uniform and a house system.   Some
freedom."*

A radical change is going to be needed to get a learning system
fit for a democracy. It needs to get away from domination and
its endless stream of uninvited teaching. It needs to recognise
that, in a democracy, learning by compulsion means
indoctrination and that only learning by invitation and choice is
education. So, it needs to be personalised in the sense of being
learner-managed, based on invitation and encouragement and, if
we actually believe in life-long learning, non-ageist. It needs to
be democratic in at least three aspects - its organisation for
participation rather than imposition, its monitoring procedures
for the celebration of learning rather than incessant and
stultifying testing, and in its adoption of the more natural
Catalogue Curriculum approach.

For the benefit of those who claim that this is all just impossible
dreams, we already have, as we have seen, a democratic learning
institution in our midst based on these principles. It is called the
public library system. There are others, such as museums,
nursery centres, home-based education networks/co-operatives
and Community Arts programmes. So we already know how to
make such systems work. I even know just a few schools that
are attempting to work to these principles, as far as the mass
coercive system allows. The most successful form of genuine
education available for children at present, however, is home-
based education, and, unsurprisingly, these families usually
make a bee-line for their local democratic learning institution –
the public library.

The present domination-riddled learning system is the result of the *Great Leap Backwards* of 1988 when the Thatcher government, after a power struggle in the Cabinet between traditionalists in the Department for Education and futurists in the Department for Employment led by David Young, took us back in time to the kind of schooling system of the early 1900s. The discredited idea of a National Curriculum with endless testing and aggressive inspection was re-established, and replaced more forward-looking ideas such as the Technical and Vocational Educational Initiative (TVEI) of David Young.

The first National Curriculum along with its repressive trappings, had eventually been discarded after the Chief Inspector for Schools, Edmond Holmes, wrote a book declaring it *The Tragedy of Education* in 1921. This was the system Holmes saw as stultifying teachers, debasing teaching and learning, inducing cheating by linking funding to test results, and weakening imagination, creativity, and flexibility, whilst promoting *"a profound misconception of the meaning of life"* by replacing improvement through encouragement and co-operation with ruthless competition and the allocation of blame for 'failure'.

If Britain wanted to have an education system fit for a new century, he concluded, it would have to stop telling children what to do and compelling them to do it, since this produced only passivity, lassitude, unhealthy docility or, in the stronger, more determined spirits, 'naughtiness'. Teaching had become a debased activity:

> *"In nine schools out of ten, on nine days out of ten, in nine lessons out of ten, the teacher is engaged in laying thin films of information on the surface of the child's mind and then after a brief interval he is skimming these off in order to satisfy himself that they have been duly laid."*

The view of Holmes, is similar to that of the 31% of young parents mentioned earlier, and was echoed by Bertrand Russell:

> *"There must be in the world many parents who, like the present author, have young children whom they are anxious to educate as well as possible, but reluctant to expose to the evils of existing educational institutions."*
> (On Education, *1926, page 7)*

In a cartoon of the learning system for animals, an elephant, a monkey, a fish, a tortoise, a squirrel and a seal are shown queuing up to be tested. The caption says, *'to ensure fairness, the test is the same for all of you – climb the tree!'* The idea that people with unique brains, multiple intelligences, a wide variety of learning styles, and varied background histories can be processed in a uniform, standardised learning system means that plenty of possible achievement will be stifled.

The alternative pathway for teachers is as 'guides on the side', with minimal use of the 'sage on the stage', of learner-directed learning rather than teacher-directed, of the Catalogue Curriculum not the government-devised curriculum. The absurdity of trying to defend the present obsolete, counter-productive and rights-abusing learning system was shown in a head teacher's desperate outburst to some doubting parents, *"If only you would make your home less interesting, your children would not be so bored at school."*

Such parents are forced to adopt the advice of Mark Twain – never let schooling interfere with your education! But we **could** switch to a learning system that was education and not schooling, and one that was fit for a modern democracy.

In the meantime, plenty of home-based educators, (though necessarily not those who have created 'school at home', thus copying many of the errors of the mass, coercive schooling system itself), have adopted a learner-managed form of personalised education and have stumbled across part of a learning system fit for a democracy.

It was in 1977 that I first began to look into home-based education with my own young son in mind. My wife Shirley, who a few years later died of cancer, was probably the best teacher of infants I had seen in my travels around schools. Then, my own teaching, first in secondary schools and then in teacher education, was well rated by others. But as two 'successful' teachers, with our insider knowledge, we knew the severe limitations of school-based education. So we began to look into the possibility of educating at home, only to stumble on the birth of *Education Otherwise* and its founding group of a few other parents thinking along the same lines as ourselves.

Soon after that I found myself in court as an expert witness supporting Iris and Geoff Harrison and their family, and their right to home-educate using the autonomous approach of *'I will do it my way - using the help and support of others as necessary'*, rather that the authoritarian approach of *'you will do it our way – or else'* of the mass, coercive schooling system.

So, I became an 'educational double agent' and for about fifteen years, some of my time was spent in teacher education, preparing post-graduate students for a career in schools, and some of my time was spent researching and supporting families who chose to educate their children at home.

Since I have always argued for a more flexible, diverse and personalised learning system, I saw no necessary contradiction in the double agent role. But others, wedded to the orthodoxy of the mass coercive schooling system, were disturbed by it.

Partly, this is due to the fact that home-based education tends to expose, rather starkly, the severe limitations of the schooling system and the damage it inflicts. This damage starts with forcing the surrender of the influence of the family to be handed over to a group of so-called 'professionals', whose training and awareness is frequently limited to the crowd instruction and crowd control form of education. The damage continues with the second surrender to the tyranny of the peer group. The system requires that the constructive approach of those families seeking to create a better world, is gradually replaced with the fatalistic 'toughen them up for real life in the nasty competitive world' philosophy. Only in home-based education does the family begin to 'strike back'.

Despite my social scientist's cautious approach to appraising the home-based learning I was seeing, the distinction between the two learning systems - school-based learning and home-based learning - became clear. The contrast between school-based and home-based education has been likened to that between factory farming and the free-range option. The consequence is that young people educated at home are usually far more mature than their schooled counterparts. I realised after a while that I could spot the difference within minutes of meeting a young person for the first time. Home-educated young people did not treat me as if I was a potential enemy and conversed with me with ease and poise, on serious as well as trivial matters.

Recently, I have been present when panels of young people who have been educated at home and are now adults, have been telling audiences about their experiences. It has been a cheering and positive event. One young person told of how he decided perhaps he should do some examinations and try university, since the message all around him in society was that this was worthwhile and the way to go. After a term of low-level misery at university, he reflected that what he really enjoyed was his part-time boat-building activity at weekends in a friend's business. So he told his tutors he was leaving university. There was plenty of protest about how well he was doing in the courses, and disbelief that he wanted to follow a practical career, not an academic/professional one.

Others came to university late as mature students after trying various activities and occupations before selecting their careers, one as a nurse, another as a lawyer. Another declared that the only examination she had ever needed was the driving test since she ran her own successful business. If ever she needed more, she would settle down and work to get them.

The contrast between the two learning systems is also illustrated by research on the experience of those who go back into school later. Just as there are many reasons why people opt for the home-based education alternative, there are also several reasons why they may choose to opt into school again later. Some express a desire to spend additional time with friends or to make new friends, or become involved in organised sports – particularly important in the USA where sports scholarships may be on offer. Some say that the academic work is a draw by working with experts and also the facilities in science subjects. Some were drawn to the challenges of meeting peer group pressure, meeting different types of people, and having their ideas challenged. Some see personality as a factor:

> "I am an extrovert and my parents and I thought that going out to school would allow me to develop in those areas (interacting with friends and teachers and communication and leadership skills)."

The study by Michael H. Romanowski, reported in *Home School Researcher*, Volume 15, number 1, 2002, shows how most of these hopes are dashed in reality. There were 20 in-depth interviews plus other contacts with another 28 cases that formed the basis of the investigation.

Firstly, the students had to learn to adjust to the **time frame** of the school with its rigid timetable, structure, habits, rules, customs and expectations:

> *"I had to learn the system and jump through the hoops, and as a home-schooler and a free spirit who used my own standards and work and study habits – it was difficult."*

> *" ... in home school I could start at 6 am and get done by 8 am, but in school you are locked into their time frame, even though much time is wasted."*

Most did not find this adjustment to be much of a problem:

> *"I expected more difficulty with the classroom routine – sitting still, paying attention, taking turns, learning class rules, and even some of the unwritten rules that all the other students knew. However, I picked it up rather quickly ..."*

Next, the **learning process** was quite different. Students had been used to one-to-one learning situations or self-directed learning but now had to cope with large classes, multiple teachers, different teaching styles and nightly homework. It could all seem rather ponderous:

> *"Many times I felt as though the teacher was going too slow. She would continue with examples when I had already figured it out from reading the instructions. It was difficult to be patient while she helped others. I used my ability to study independently to advantage. I would get a head start on that evening's homework in the middle of the class ..."*

Another response was,

> *"A lot of time is wasted for everyone to finish their assignments in class ... It's hard when the teacher has to*

teach to the lowest common denominator. I don't think school is very challenging."

And,

"It takes so much longer to get the same amount of work done ... You don't get half the stuff done you could get done at home ... it gets boring."

The respondents in the study reported that they learnt to cope with the **slow pace of instruction**, waiting for others, wasted class time, and numerous distractions that interrupted the learning process, but they paid the price of finding their interest and motivation to learning declining. Although most indicated they thought the academic work might be difficult for them, in the event they found the opposite to be true. But they paid a different price: *"... there was no room for creativity or individual thinking".*

The learner-friendly nature of home-based education gave way to something that was more **learner-hostile**:

"It all comes back to assembly line teaching in the end ... I found myself bored and often went through the motions of learning ... I found out really quick how to get good grades without having to do hardly any work."

Earlier researchers (e.g. Smedley 1992) have proposed that home-educated people were more mature than their schooled counterparts. The respondents in this study found this to be the case:

"Many of the kids in the class were very immature."

"I felt I was much more mature than my peers ..."

"Most of the kids were immature and many are cruel ... I didn't expect the kids to act so childish."

As a result the aim of making new friends was largely thwarted.

The peer culture caused many value clashes. One centred around **cheating**. The acceptance and tolerance of cheating was a challenge to home-educated students who had been brought up on honesty. This occurred both in work and in relationships where betrayal was commonplace:

"... dealing with betrayal from people that I thought were my friends. I can't trust people. There is so much gossiping over stupid things and there is so much lying that took place. Students lie without ever considering it as being wrong."

Another issue was **language**. Home-schooled students had to learn that **profanity** was part of the accepted language of the student culture. It had a numbing effect:

"It's easy to become numb to the constant bad language and actions that go against your ideals ..."

Fighting, sex, drugs, alcohol and stealing presented other value clashes:

"Sex, drugs, stealing and doing bad things became tempting as a way to fit into the social aspects of the school ..."

The emphasis on **materialism** and **appearance** also came as a shock:

"I was not expecting clothing and appearance to be such a big deal ... if you didn't have the right clothes or look good, it was tough to fit into the 'right' crowd."

One student concluded, "I was much happier when I studied at home."

The researcher ends with the need for students going back into school to be thoroughly prepared for what lies ahead. There may be a need for a family 'damage limitation programme'.

This research does not give much of an advert for schooling and show the inmates are likely to have been kept **artificially immature** and **somewhat brutalized** by what Holt calls "the long practical course in slavery" that is school. One impressive passage in the Bible proposes that 'whatsover things are true...honest ... pure ... lovely ... of good report, if there be any virtue and if there be any praise, think on these things'. School, whether by intent or by an unrecognised process, appears to be offering almost the opposite. And there is a likely nasty payoff, if WH Auden is right when he writes that, *"Those to whom evil is done, do evil in return"*.

For children to survive within the school system, they must allow their individual personalities to be, in some cases partly, and in other cases almost completely, absorbed by the institution. They have to stop being people and become pupils, They must reduce personal learning and research, to become the subjects of endless uninvited teaching.

In contrast, consider the verdict from Robert's story (in *Home Educating Our Autistic Spectrum Children*, eds. T. Dowty and K. Cowlishaw):

> *"Thanks, Mum, for taking me out of school. I can honestly say I now enjoy living."*

'School' has had a more honourable definition in the past. When scholars (or 'schoolers') like Peter Abelard visited towns in the middle ages, a 'school' of voluntary 'seekers after truth' would form to hear and debate the latest ideas, and people of all ages would gather together for the event. (The OFSTED minded establishment did not like this very much and so asserted the one right way of seeing things by eventually declaring him a heretic and his ideas as heretical.) It is hard to imagine anything further removed from a 'voluntary gathering of seekers after truth' that the mass, coercive school.

Can we imagine a world without schools? Gerald Haigh, former head teacher and now journalist for the *Times Education Supplement* thinks we can:

> *"Fanciful nonsense? Don't be so sure. My grandparents knew about workhouses. An accepted part of the social landscape for centuries, they now seem impossibly inhumane and counterproductive. One day, school will be seen like that – a transient phenomenon, destined to fade gracefully away as the forces that created them gradually lose their impetus."*

(from 'Goodbye to today's workhouses', *Times Educational Supplement 21/1/05*)

And so, in conclusion, I return to my letter to *the Times Educational Supplement* which I referred to in chapter 7.   I ended that letter with a challenge:

> *"Let's be a bit bolder than trying to make yesterday's tired and failed idea of mass schooling work!"*

The challenge remains relevant and, with the passing of time, it becomes increasingly urgent.   If we want a learning system fit for humans in a democracy, we have to face up to the stark proposition that ... **school is not the solution, it is part of the problem.**

Selected References and Further Reading

Bartholomew, J. (1976) 'Schooling Teachers: The Myth of the Liberal College', in Whitty, G. and Young, M.F.D. (1976) *Explorations in the Politics of Knowledge*, Driffield: Nafferton Books.

Buttress, D. (2004) *Broxtowe Boy*, Nottingham: Shoestring Press.

Chamberlin, R. (1989) *Free Children and Democratic Schools*, London: Falmer.

Davies, L. (1994) *Beyond Authoritarian School Management*, Ticknall: Education Now Books.

Engle, S. and Ochoa, A. (1989) *Education for Democratic Citizenship*, Columbia: Teachers College Press.

Friere, P. (1972) *Pedagogy of the Oppressed*, Harmondsworth: Penguin.

Gordon, T. (1986) *Democracy in One School?*, London: Falmer.

Harber, C., and Meighan, R., (1989) *The Democratic School: educational management and the practice of democracy*, Ticknall: Education Now Books.

Harber, C. (1995) *Developing Democratic Education*, Ticknall: Education Now Books.

Hart R. (1992) *Children's Participation from Tokenism to Citizenship Innocenti Essuyu No. 4*, UNICEF. London.

Keefe, J.W. (1987) *Learning Style Theory and Practice*, Reston, VA: NASSP.

Kelly, A.V. (1995) *Education and Democracy*, London: Paul Chapman.

Kohl, H. (1970) *The Open Classroom*, London: Methuen.

Meighan, R. - a list of relevant books is given on the Dedication page.

Nicholls, J. G. (1989) *The Competitive Ethos and Democratic Education*, Cambridge Massachusetts: Harvard Univ. Press.

Rogers, C. (1983) *Freedom to Learn for the Eighties*, Colombus: Ohio: Merrill.

Russell, B. (1926) *On Education*, London: George Allen and Unwin

Trafford, B. (1997) *Participation, Power-sharing and School Improvement*, Nottingham: Educational Heretics Press.

Watts, J. (1980) *Towards an Open School*, London: Longman.

Webster, M. and Buglass, G. (2005) *Finding Voices, Making Choices*, Nottingham: Educational Heretics Press

White, P. (1983) *Beyond Domination*, London: Routledge and Kegan Paul.

Activities

In the introduction is a list of learning systems. Some have been selected as case studies. The others are all available for analysis.

For example, you can choose from the Scouts and Guides, The Duke of Edinburgh's Award Scheme, Summerhill School, Sands School, any Public School, any Independent School, The Open University, any traditional University, the Met campuses USA, Steiner schools, Montessori schools, and Sudbury Valley school USA.

The lists of key characteristics used in chapters 3,4,5 and 6 will give you a start.

Selected Index

Adcock, John 83
Abbott, John 79
Aims of education 2, 9, 13, 38
Alexander, Rob 86
Alternatives in education 8, 58
Assessment 9, 13, 38, 83
Auden, W.H. 110
Authoritarian learning 5, 9-13, 58
Autonomous learning 5, 15-36

Baldaro, James 48, 49-52
Ball, Christopher 7, 79, 83, 91
Barson, Leslie 56
Bengu, Professor 102
Benn, Tony 99
Bonner, Sonia 48
Brain research 2, 3, 26, 100
Browne, Lesley 48, 52-54
Bruner, Jerome 4
Bullying 25, 36, 80
- institutions 6, 10, 80
- mentality 25
Buttress, Derrick 30-34
Bulman, Tom 66

Catalogue curriculum 21-2, 82-3, 94, 105
Centre
- for self-managed learning 16, 87
- for personalised education 16
Choice in education 98
Churchill, Winston 58
Citischool 66
City as school 66-8
Community Arts 29, 69-75
Community learning centres 29, 82
Competition v. co-operation 7
Cultural mechanics 19
Cunningham, Ian 16, 87
Curriculum
- catalogue 21-2, 82-3, 94, 105
- hidden 77
- imposed 4
- National 3, 4, 10-13, 60,104
- natural 3-4

Damage limitation 78
Default position of learning systems 59
Democratic learning 5, 10, 11, 37-56
- in schools 48-55
-pre-democratic 99
Department for Education and Skills 96
Department for the Encouragement of Learning 97
Discipline 9, 15, 23-4, 37, 57-9
Domination, absence of 102, 103

Ellis, William 79
Existential questions 3-4

First-hand experiences 23
Fit for purpose 2
Flexi-time schooling 89
Friar, Linda 88

Gardner, Howard 22
Gatto, John Taylor 3, 30, 80
Genius, studies of 7
Glines, Don 6, 36, 62, 82
Goodman, Paul 94, 101
Group learning contracts 39

Haigh, Gerald 111
Hall, E.T. 3
Harber, Clive 39, 52, 53
Hemming, James 101
Hepple, Stephen 35
High Scope project 20
Holmes, Edmond 8, 20, 60, 93, 96, 104
Holt, John 4, 77, 97, 99, 110
Home-based education 7, 8, 11, 17-27, 82, 85-7, 91, 100-1, 105
Hostile learning environments 19, 109

Ideologies of education 4-6
Indoctrination 103
Information-rich society 17-18, 100
Intentions 2
Interactionist learning systems 5, 57-76
Isle of Wight Learning Zone 86-7

Key stages 13
Knowledge 9, 13, 37

Leadership 38

Learning
- coaches 22
- co-operatives 39
- episodes 94-8
- styles 18, 100
- travel agent 83
Learners as researchers 35
Learner-managed learning 20, 81, 93-8
Liberal regimes 5
Life-long learning 16
Location 9, 13, 37

Mandela, Nelson 102
Mankato Wilson School 62-5
McCurdy, H.G. 7-8
Meaning of life 8
Meighan, Roland 39, 52, 53, 60
Mills, C. Wright 20
Moore, Patrick 97
Multiple intelligences 22, 100

National Curriculum 3, 4,10-13, 60, 104
Natural learning 2, 3, 17
Needle, Nat 6, 7
Notschool.net 35-6

Oliver, Kate 89-90
Organisation 9, 13, 37
Otherwise Club 56, 85-86

Papert, Seymour 83
Parents 9, 13, 37
Parkway project 66
Peer culture 109-10
Personalised learning 16, 62, 64, 93-8, 103, 110
Plan, Do, Review 20
Power 9, 13, 38
- sharing 99
Pre-democratic 99
Progressive education 59
Public library 28-34, 97, 103

Regressive education 59
Reimer, Everett 94
Resources 9, 13, 37
Rogers, Carl 55
Rose, Colin and Nicholl, Malcolm 26
Russell, Bertrand 2, 59, 104

Sands School 55
School
- coercive 58
- compulsory 4, 103
- convivial 58
Skills 13
Social skills 34
South Downs Learning Centre 87-8
Stables Project 88-9
Subjects 12
Sudbury Valley School 55

Teaching 9, 13, 37, 45
- uninvited 13, 103, 110
Time, use of 19
Totalitarian regimes and learning 5, 10, 99, 102
Trafford, Bernard 60
Twain, Mark 105

Understanding 13
Uninvited teaching 13, 103, 110
Uppattinas Centre 90-1

Virtual school 66

Walsall Community Arts Team 72
Webster, Mark 69
William 32-33
Wolverhampton Grammar School 61
Wragg, Ted 101, 102-3

Year-round education 63